The
HOLLOW Tree

HOL

The
L**O**W

Tree

Fighting Addiction with Traditional Native Healing

Herb Nabigon

McGILL-QUEEN'S UNIVERSITY PRESS

Montreal & Kingston · London · Chicago

ISBN 978-0-7735-3132-1 (paper)
ISBN 978-0-7735-7625-4 (ePDF)
ISBN 978-0-7735-7880-7 (ePUB)

Legal deposit third quarter 2006
Bibliothèque nationale du Québec

Reprinted 2007, 2010, 2014, 2016, 2021, 2023

Printed in Canada on acid-free paper that is 100% ancient forest free
(100% post-consumer recycled), processed chlorine free.

Funded by the Government of Canada   Financé par le gouvernement du Canada   Canada   Canada Council for the Arts   Conseil des arts du Canada

We acknowledge the support of the Canada Council for the Arts.

Nous remercions le Conseil des arts du Canada de son soutien.

Library and Archives Canada Cataloguing in Publication

Nabigon, Herb
The hollow tree : fighting addiction with traditional native healing /
Herb Nabigon; illustrations by Leo Yerxa.

(McGill-Queen's Indigenous and northern studies; no. 49)
ISBN 978-0-7735-3132-1 (paper)
ISBN 978-0-7735-7625-4 (ePDF)
ISBN 978-0-7735-7880-7 (ePUB)

1. Nabigon, Herb – Alcohol use. 2. Alcoholism – Treatment –
Canada. 3. Indians of North America – Canada – Religion.
4. Indians of North America – Canada – Rites and ceremonies.
5. Indians of North America – Canada – Biography. 6. Spiritual
healing. I. Title. II. Series.

E78.C2N23 2006   362.292'08997071   C2006-902159-7

This book was designed and typeset by
studio oneonone in Sabon 10/14.5

This book is dedicated to Sheila, the mother of our two children, Clem and Alana, and to my youngest son, Danny Jones. It is also dedicated to all my brothers and sisters who still suffer with substance addictions. I pray the latter will find guidance to walk the red path.

Contents

Foreword

GEORGES SIOUI

We often hear or read the words: "It is both an honour and a pleasure to be asked by so and so to say (or write) a few words because he/she did such and such valuable thing, etc." Well, this foreword that my great friend Herb Nabigon asked me to write for his book, *The Hollow Tree*, comes with an extraspecial feeling. At some very important turning points in our respective lives, Herb and I walked side by side as the brothers that we are. As Herb amply and eloquently explains throughout his book, our revered Elders and *Mushums* (Grand-fathers), Eddy Bellerose, Abe Burnstick, and others, used all the love contained in their hearts to make us see and be thankful for the great beauty of our Ancestors' spiritual legacy as well as for our responsibility to share these gifts with our sisters and brothers who have come to live with us on our land.

This book is destined to shine as an example of the power of our Elders to use their spiritual gifts to turn their people away from unbalanced life ways and self-destructive feelings such as hate, resentment, inferiority, and jealousy towards a life guided by kindness, honesty, courage, and humility. At a time when I was confused and needed a helping hand and a voice of wisdom and love from one of my own people, Herb gave me his hand and led me to our Elders. I will always recall the brotherly care he used in enticing me to take those very important first steps against my own foolish will (I thought that I knew almost everything about my culture when in fact I knew very little; besides, I could not imagine then a life without alcohol). That time, in March 1980, Herb made me listen, and, along with our other great friend Roy Thomas and several others, we went to a week-long cultural awareness workshop given by the Alberta Elders whom I have already named. Why I have never touched alcohol since I went to that workshop I will never really be able to explain. I can only give thanks for the beautiful gifts I received from the Great Spirit through the Elders' and Herb's hands.

Now, I would like to give one other especially convincing proof of the far-reaching power of recovering our spiritual traditions. This is a true revelation about a very well-known legal case, the *Sioui* case (*Sioui vs Regina*, Supreme Court of Canada, May 1990). Herb and I have not disclosed until now that our eviction in May 1982 from the Parc des Laurentides in Quebec, on the third day of our spiritual fast, was the genesis of the *Sioui* case, an important legal victory for my four brothers and myself on behalf of our Huron-Wendat Nation. As ordered by the park authorities, we left the site of our fast that day, but the legal defence we undertook, which lasted for the next eight years, led to a unanimous decision by Canada's

Supreme Court in our favour, a momentous victory for all of Canada's Aboriginal Nations and their citizens. And the essential truth of the matter is that without the teachings received from our Elders three years before, in the Kootenay Plains in Alberta, we would not have had the ability to infuse new life into an old document, long since considered obsolete, that our Nation had preserved for the past 230 years and that was now (thanks to the Elder's teachings) finally recognized by Quebec and Canada as a *treaty*! Without our learning from the Elders (our Holy People), we would not have undertaken, let alone won that legal-spiritual battle.

(Not being a resident of Quebec, Herb was not prosecuted, but we, the Sioui brothers, jokingly explain his absence from the legal picture by saying that there was an Ojibway there with us, but as soon as he saw the Conservation officers coming, he took off through the woods, making a beeline for his northern Ontario home and apparently was never seen again!)

In the twenty-five years of friendship that we share, I have seen my "Neechee" Herb Nabigon walk away from the doom of alcohol, hurt, and despair to the place of high respectability, personal balance, and collective hope reflected in his status as a university professor and his recognition as an Elder among his Niishnaabe people and our Aboriginal nations. When I think of the strong, beautiful, fun person that my friend is, I feel deep gratitude and love for the Elders (including Herb's parents and forebears) who have salvaged him from alcohol's unforgiving grip and given him back to us, his relatives, as a brother and a teacher. Herb's experience and salvation through Aboriginal spirituality are a powerful illustration of the grave loss incurred by First Nations people every time one of their own is annihilated through addiction to alcohol and other substances. Herb's cruel alcoholic ordeal and his return to wholeness through reconnection with his own Aboriginal spirituality are also evidence that the simple nature-based spiritual beliefs and practices taught by traditional spiritual Elders possess important healing power for all people, because all people have and need the same connection to Nature.

Herb, I will always be your affectionate friend.

GEORGES SIOUI
Coordinator, Native Studies Program
University of Ottawa

Foreword

ZORICA BENKOVIC

First Nations people of this country, and indeed many people from various other cultures, have countless stories to tell of their own personal struggles in breaking free from addiction. For some, the decision to stop "using" came the hard way, in a jail cell or through an accident. For others, healing arose from the ultimatums given to them by their family members who threatened to leave or by their employers who threatened to take away their job. Whatever the circumstances may be, the process of recovering from an addiction is a personal decision ... a choice.

The question "Why do so many people abuse alcohol or drugs?" is a common query for which there is no simple answer. The further question why some individuals are more successful than others in their attempts to stop using alcohol or drugs is just as difficult to answer. In this book, Herb writes of the pain and suffering he went through in freeing himself from alcoholism. He tells us about the many choices he made throughout his life (some good and some not so good) and how these choices affected him both as a person and, more importantly, as an Aboriginal.

Whenever I read a book of this nature I ask myself a few simple questions. Does the book provide the reader with enough information to identify with? Will the book do more than just educate the reader on the issues? Will it provide readers with suggestions as to how they can better their our lives? More importantly, does the story consist solely of technical academic lingo that will more than likely alienate the readers who need it the most or is it easy to follow? With respect to *The Hollow Tree*, the answer to these questions is yes. In the following pages you will find no guilt trips, no burdens, no demands. Herb's story is much more powerful than the series of steps or procedures we often find in self-help literature.

This book is about accepting responsibility, making choices, and being honest with ourselves. Although most of the content in *The Hollow Tree* deals with First Nations struggles in healing from alcohol abuse, it also provides a framework for those of us who are not Native so that we too can discover the traditional healing methods found in Native cultures.

The real pleasure here is that we can take these healing concepts and build better relationships at home, at work, or in school. We can share these concepts with others and bring healing not only unto ourselves but to our brothers, sisters, parents, aunties, uncles, and ultimately, our communities.

ZORICA BENKOVIC
Centre for Research in Human Development
Laurentian University

Acknowledgments

This book would not have been possible if the Elders and Teachers of Four Skies Consulting had not shown me how to embark upon my own spiritual journey. Eddy Bellerose and Abe Burnstick (both now deceased), and a senior Elder, also deceased, who wishes to remain anonymous, literally saved my sanity with their wisdom and caring and made it possible for me to share this experience with others.

Dr Rebecca Hagey provided editorial comments, and Gary Schaan offered valuable suggestions about inclusions for clarification.

Louise McCallum, for typing the manuscript, is gratefully appreciated and acknowledged. Also Heather Campbell provided valuable guidance and suggestions for further clarification.

Miigwech gzhemnidoo kina bemaadzijig.
Thank-you Great Spirit and all the people.

HERB NABIGON
2003

Introduction

The hollow tree is a metaphor for what Western culture has become, an empty shell with no substance. That greed and selfishness rule and that we have little regard for our neighbours demonstrates how unbalanced we are as a people. The hollow tree also identifies individuals who make up our society. Many people's misuse of power continues to cause suffering in the world. But, as Art Solomon says in his poem *There Is No Middle Ground*, it is time that you do something about you. It is time to remember our sacred connections, to transform that hollow tree into the sacred tree it was meant to be, to take responsibility for our individual lives and to act upon it, so that we may follow our path with our hearts. Perhaps then our forest of people will be healthy and grow beings who can live in harmony, side by side.

Our society can balance itself if more emphasis is placed upon spirituality in our everyday lives, for without spirituality we will perish. We will perish if we continue to over-emphasize the rational and logical sides of life, forgetting the need for balance. The result will be more pollution,

consumerism, and disregard for our relationship with the Earth. Honest and kind faith will transform "hollow trees" into caring, balanced beings.

The colour blue surrounding the hollow tree represents the sky world. The Creator and her spirit-helpers live in the sky world. The colours below the tree represent traditional teachings that we use to fill the hollow tree and transform ourselves. It follows that society will be transformed into a more caring community. The teachings give us the power to transform ourselves. The colours of the roots are yellow, red, black, and white. We must draw out energy from the four directions.

The sacred pipe depicted among the colours represents a tool we use to communicate with the Creator. The stem is made of wood, which represents honesty. The bowl is made of rock representing spiritual strength, and tobacco represents kindness.

The
HOLLOW

Tree

The Heart Can Heal

The heart can heal
what the mind betrays
But only the soul
can free the man

Oh soul of mine
release my fears
Abide in me again
like in yesteryears
When life was sacred
and death far, far away

Oh soul of mine
walk with me awhile
till the strength returns
and my heart heals
Hold me in tender embrace
and erase my fears

Oh soul of mine
Abide in me again
Just for a little while
till my heart be strong
And my mind be calm
of all life's fears

Oh most Sacred Soul, the Great Wonder
Uncage this man
Let freedom thunder
in his life once more.

Ovide Mercredi, 12 January 1999
Former Chief of the Assembly of First Nations

The Early Years

This is a story of hope, and how I healed myself of fear, loneliness, and conflict within my mind, body, and spirit. Many times I tried to resolve these feelings and conflicts through the use of alcohol – preferably a bottle of whiskey. But no matter how hard I tried, my problems just seemed to get larger in scale. I got to a point where I was not aware of how warped my thinking had become. The difference between good and bad was a blur and I no longer understood what was just or unjust. Alcohol was destroying my life and I did not know it.

My name is Herb Nabigon. I was born on Pic Mobert First Nation, in Ontario, on 16 July 1942. My father, Clem, was a trapper who provided for our family by living off the land. I wanted so much to be like Dad. I remember learning how to set beaver traps and rabbit snares with him. When we were young, Dad was always busy on his trapline, spending the long winters away from the reserve. He was a man of strong spirit who was very close to nature. My mother, Mabel, a gentle woman, gave birth to three children. In those days there were a lot of good feelings in our home. Mom always insisted that we had enough to eat, dry clothing, and a lot of affection ... balance and love were characteristic of our family.

When I turned nine years old, like many other Native children, I was taken from my parents and sent to a Residential School in Spanish, Ontario. These schools were established by the federal government as part of a plan to assimilate Native peoples into the Western culture. In the 1850s an act that made it mandatory that Native children be removed from their families was implemented. This act, called the Indian Act, was established to remove the traditional values and beliefs from our culture, forcing Western values upon our people. The policy of assimilation in the 1950s forbid the spiritual teachings of fasting, pipe, and sweatlodge ceremonies. The policy of outlawing our spiritual beliefs and language had a devastating affect on our identities as Native people. Many Native people left the Christian churches (Roman Catholic, Anglican, United Church, ect.) as a result of this policy.

This prescriptive and intrusive policy devastated parents and children alike. No longer would parents have any control over their children's lives. Children as young as six years old would be taken from their homes and placed in a school, often far from their homes, where their names would be replaced by numbers. They were completely stripped of their past identity and punished for speaking their Native tongue. This was the setting for the many triggers in my life that led me on a downward spiral of despair.

I remember when I was about twelve years old, I wanted to be a hero and save other people, like the Lone Ranger in the radio broadcast series. I never wanted to be like his sidekick, Tonto, because Native people viewed him as a sell-out, a yes-man of the Western culture and their patriarchal thinking. I must have been aware of the devastation of many people's lives around me, because I really wanted to be that "lone ranger hero." In my youth I did not take into consideration the many twists and turns that we confront on our path in life. I soon found, as a young adult, that the illusion I had of achieving heroic victories was far beyond my reach. An Elder of Wisdom would have been good company in those days and the many dark days to follow. I was "a-lone" and my dreams gave new meaning to the "range" of despair I would soon touch.

I took my first drink of wine when I was in high school. All I can remember is getting really sick and passing out. Somehow, it eased the pain of being away from my family. I felt like one of those hollow trees you see in the bush that is desperately trying to survive the natural elements. I didn't know how to handle alcohol, but at the time I thought that it was the best thing that I had ever had. Like a magic elixir, it gave me courage and made me feel so good about myself that I was not afraid to speak up to these unfriendly people who produced feelings of inferiority within me. After having a couple of these magical drinks, my apprehensions seemed to disappear. I was no longer crippled by the fear within that had created an empty cavity in my chest.

The first time I had to deal with inner conflict was in 1957. I was fourteen years old and I had returned home from school, located in North Bay, to visit my family during March break. My mother was in the hospital and no one had told me she was dying. The shock was so powerful that my only thought was to escape the devastation and get back to school. I wanted to run away from the pain of seeing my mother in this condition. Not long after my return to school that spring, I was called back to the reserve to attend her burial in Mobert.

I did not feel much compassion for myself over the loss of my mother. I preferred to sweep the numbing pain away as if it had never happened. I remember enjoying the experience of having my relatives and friends offer their condolences and paying special attention to my suffering. But deep down inside I felt lousy, for I was using my mother's funeral to gain sympathy and recognition for myself. The grief, guilt, and shame of a lonely, confused child added contempt to that empty feeling in my chest. My need to manipulate people's unconditional love to justify my own hurt controlled me for many, many years.

I was in turmoil and spoke to no one about the anguish that I was experiencing. I began to avoid dealing with this pain in my newly accustomed manner. The night after my mother was buried I drank myself into oblivion. The guilt that I had felt about using my mother's death for my own personal gain and the lack of courage to share my deception with others consumed me. Shortly after my mother died I realized that these inner conflicts and feelings of inferiority were crushing me and I quit school. I did not recognize it then, but I was setting a pattern for myself that was to cause me indescribable pain and suffering for years to come. As I see it now, by avoiding my pain, by running away from it, I had increased its power over me almost to the point of self destruction.

In 1959, at age seventeen, I obtained a job with the railway as a station agent. This job suited me well. I was still basking in the illusion of the importance of power and my position fulfilled this illusion perfectly. Most of my friends worked outside in construction, and I felt that my job gave me special status. I was working indoors. I was a big shot because I had control over the destination of others. Anyone who wanted to travel by train had to obtain a ticket from me! While I was with the railway, my illusion of having power fed upon itself and my drinking became progressively worse. My intake of alcohol increased at the expense of my nutritional well-being. My hangovers were getting unbearable and my nerves became jittery. I lacked understanding and I couldn't see through the veil of smoke that the alcohol had created. I was unaware of the power it had over me and I began to think like a crazy man.

When I drank I felt powerful and in control. I felt that I was above the rules and regulations that the other railway workers had to abide by. Nothing could happen to me. I had special status. Once, my uncle mentioned that he wanted to take a trip on a train and I wilfully loaned him my railway pass, something that was strictly against company policy. He was caught in Sudbury, Ontario, and I was fired because of my irresponsible behaviour. My father was very angry with me. I had lost my job, but I really didn't care. My basic attitude was easy come, easy go. I wasn't even slightly disturbed by the fact that I had ruined my chances for a potential career with the Canadian Pacific

Railway. The world around us was changing and the traditional lifestyle of the Native people was rapidly dissipating. My father understood the importance of gaining a solid position with a company like the CPR, but I was unaware of its significance. This carefree, irresponsible mindset continued to create problems for me.

After being fired from the railway, I drifted around Mobert for about a year doing odd jobs – tree planting, construction, whatever it took to support my habit. Yet as I continued to lark around the reserve, something inside was eating at me. I was not satisfied with this lifestyle. Boldly I applied for a job with the Canadian National Railway in Hornepayne, Ontario, and to my surprise, I got the position.

My first assignment was to work as an operator and station agent in Longlac, Ontario. Conveniently, my grandmother was living in Longlac at the time and I moved in with her. My job with the CNR lasted for about a year and a half before my drinking began to take control again. One evening, while I was working the graveyard shift, my friend Evelyn brought over a twenty-sixer of rye. After we had had a couple of drinks I began to feel quite confident and at about two o'clock in the morning I decided, in my drunken arrogance and against all regulations, to close the station. I locked up and we went over to my bunkhouse where we continued to party. At three o'clock that morning a freight train arrived at the station but the driver could not go any further because there was no operator to give him clearance. In my negligence I delayed the train and its entire crew for about three hours. Meanwhile, with the heroic lone ranger missing in action, CNR management found a competent replacement.

The next morning I was roughly awakened by the CNR police and instructed to report to head office immediately. I took the next train out of Longlac and reported to my boss in Hornepayne.

"You had a good career here with the CNR and you blew it because of drinking. What are you going to do with yourself?" he asked.

So what? I thought. Who needs a career? There are a lot of jobs out there. I don't really need a career. All I need is more money to drink. I felt little, if any, remorse for my action at Longlac. My boss's lecture had no effect on me. It had gone in one ear and out the other. That drunken episode had cost me yet another job.

It was easy to find excuses in those days. Self-justification accusations came automatically. In my mind my dismissal from the CNR was caused solely by the personal prejudices of my boss. He's only firing me because I'm an Indian. He really didn't have to fire me, he could have put me on suspension for violating Rule G of the railway manual. Firing me was a little harsh! At that time I began to think that the whole world was against me. Blaming other people for my own actions was my way of problem solving.

I didn't bother going back home to pack my clothes or to bid my grandmother goodbye. I just left. My only thought was that I had to get out of Hornepayne. But where would I go? I tossed a coin, leaving my destination to fate. This was how I made decisions in those days – "heads," I go to Toronto, "tails," I go to Winnipeg. The coin said "heads," so I caught the next train to Toronto.

When I arrived in Toronto I had no idea what I was going to do, nor did I care. Luckily for me I had some cousins who were working for a construction company there. They welcomed me with open arms and I moved into their basement apartment, on Bedford Avenue, where I stayed for about two months. While I was in Toronto, I drank a lot of draft beer and got a job as a dockworker for a trucking firm. My job was to load and unload freight from trucks onto boxcars. The hard work kept me very thirsty and our first priority was to buy our beer and then to pay the rent with whatever money that was left. Food and nourishment were the farthest things from our minds, just secondary considerations and inconveniences.

After about six weeks in Toronto, I quit my job and decided to go back to Mobert. I was just drifting. In Mobert I resumed my life of delinquency and continued to party. Of course Dad was not too pleased to see me home in this condition, virtually unemployed and unconcerned about my future. He had once told me that aside from murder and rape, the worst crime a human being can commit is to destroy his or her mind with alcohol and break the natural cycle of life. I listened to his words of wisdom but they had no meaning for me. I didn't have the slightest notion of what he meant by "the natural cycle of life." I was clearly on the road to self-destruction. I was an ignorant moron – only I was the last to figure it out.

At the age of twenty I began to notice the lack of close friends and female companions in my life. Something was wrong, but I didn't know what it was. Something was eating away inside of me and the only way I knew how to handle it was to drink more whiskey. I didn't know how to express myself and my problems were intensified because of my inability to find the words to describe what I was feeling. When I did express my opinion I continually blamed others for my problems. I didn't know how to take responsibility for my own actions and I never seriously looked for any solutions. I was constantly running from myself. This was an indication of the seriousness of my mental state. I didn't know how to use my mind for positive growth. My emotions confused me and in my weakened frame of mind I was disoriented. I had no sense of direction and felt no reason to change my reckless lifestyle. I went about my daily routine in a state of numbness.

The date 4 August 1962 will remain with me forever. The day before, I had gone to White River to party with some friends, and I drank all night. The next morning, still drinking quite heavily, I went to visit my grandfather, and by noon on the fourth I had blacked out. I have no recollection of how the accident happened. To this day I wonder whether the train ran over my arm as I lay beside the track, or whether my arm was caught by a part of the train and torn from my body because I was standing too close to it as it hurtled by. Perhaps it had happened another way? I do not know. I vaguely remember talking to people standing all around me after the accident as I lay beside the track, but I cannot recall what was said. Apparently, I was told much later, my sister Dorothy found me. On 5 August I woke up in Marathon Hospital without my right arm.

It did not dawn on me that I had lost my arm until about three weeks later. One day, while I was lying in my hospital bed, the sudden realization that my arm was gone forever hit me. Deep depression engulfed me. My life was over. I felt completely hopeless. I had nothing more to live for. Soon my depression turned to anger. The anger consumed me and I became obnoxious towards my immediate family, the nursing staff, and the doctors who were caring for me. The only way I could relate to people was to tell them how I felt that the world had screwed me up. This anger stayed with me for many years and eventually the hostility tore me apart.

After the accident, almost without exception, everyone I had contact with showed compassion for me. They knew that I was in for a rough time but I reacted by rejecting their compassion. I thought that they just felt sorry for me and somehow I could not bring myself to trust people, to believe that they really had my best interests at heart, that they could be relied upon to help me with my life. I now realize that, during my stay in Marathon Hospital, my old habits of manipulating people resurfaced and intensified. Whenever I asked someone for something, cigarettes, spending money, clothing, even little things like chocolate bars, they brought them to me on demand. I found that I could manipulate their empathy for my own greedy purposes. They would do these things for me out of sympathy or guilt and I translated their gestures into a little gold mine. Instead of being able to receive their care and being grateful for it, my philosophy became: "I will get what I want through their compassion and use people for my own selfish desires." My skewed thinking caused me to believe that people's feelings were not genuine. I had bought into a false teaching and acted in this way because I felt that I didn't deserve the concern of others. The little child within me had not learned anything from his past experiences.

Looking back on it now, I realize that during my hospital stay the nurses and doctors were extremely kind to me. They swayed gently around me like sweetgrass on a warm day. Doctor Reason was an excellent surgeon. He saved my life. Were it not for his skill I would not be here today. A nurse by the name of Betty-Ann encouraged me to learn how to write again. Before my accident I had been right-handed. Now I had to learn a whole new way of doing things. Even the little everyday chore of getting dressed had become a major challenge. I have never really thanked Nurse Betty-Ann for her reassurance and wisdom until now. *Miigwech* Betty-Ann. I am grateful for the caring you provided me in my time of despair.

When I was released from the hospital I moved in with my father and stayed with him for about a year. I continued to enjoy many parties, followed by many bad hangovers. My health was deteriorating fast. One day my father found me lying beside some railway tracks, stone drunk. I was getting worse. The loss of my arm hadn't stopped me from drinking. Alcohol had complete and absolute power over me. This is the true nature of alcoholism.

My father did his best to help me recover but he began

to realize that he was only encouraging my bad habits by allowing me to stay at home and by not demanding any responsibility from me. He gave me a choice: I could either sober up or I could leave. Naturally, I chose the latter alternative because I certainly did not want to quit drinking. I left my home and moved back to Toronto.

This time I took advantage of an opportunity to go to school and work on getting my grade twelve education. I met many good people at school. They did their best to provide me with the support and encouragement that I needed to make something of myself, but I was not ready to listen. I was too busy trying to find meaning and substance in my life at the bottom of a bottle of firewater. I now needed my "friend" to function on a daily basis. Within two years I finished my Manpower Retraining Program and got a job with the Department of Public Works as a mailboy. I thought it was a great job because it didn't demand much responsibility from me and I could continue drinking without too much harassment from the boss.

A couple of years later, I met an old friend from Thunder Bay who introduced me to the organization known as the Company of Young Canadians (CYC). In the spring of 1968 I became a summer volunteer. I met bright young articulate Ojibway people who were interested in helping their communities achieve some self-sufficiency without the aid of government handouts. They were interested in social change and I liked their ideas. They wanted to see Indian communities take control of themselves and become independent of the Department of Indian Affairs and other government agencies. Intellectually, I supported their aspirations wholeheartedly. I had every intention of striving towards the same goals and becoming actively involved with the Indian community in the region. But I was inexperienced. I didn't know anything about government, politics, or the economy. The only thing I knew was that Native peoples living both on and off the reserves were poor. I asked myself, "Why?" Since I was a problem drinker, I already had a lot of unresolved anger within me and the sudden realization of the injustice of reserve poverty made me see red. It added fuel to the fire and helped me to justify my drinking.

The Company of Young Canadians had no plan of action for dealing with these issues, but we were determined to do something about them. I was assigned, along with several other young people at CYC, to start a local radio program for the surrounding reserves. During our training period, we were sent to Edmonton, Alberta, to interview Indian leaders in the area. During that time I continued to drink heavily. There seemed to be an endless supply of alcohol and I was in my glory.

While in Edmonton, I spent my time drinking. I had a very low opinion of myself to begin with so I didn't even bother to check out the possibility of interviewing any leaders. I thought that they would be too busy to talk to a guy like me. I spent three weeks in Edmonton, socializing and finding any excuse to drink. I wasn't the least bit concerned about the day that I would have to return home. When I did return, I returned without any interviews. The only recordings I had on tape were some songs by Hank Williams, which I handed over to my boss.

I got into serious trouble with the CYC management over that move. Shortly after, I acquired the disgraceful distinction of being, to the best of my knowledge, the only Indian in Canada to have been fired by the CYC. Once again I found myself unemployed with no place to go. The only things I knew were alcohol, school, and a little community organizational work that I had done with the CYC. I decided to pursue the second area of my experience and I returned to school. I enrolled in a two-year social services diploma program in Thunder Bay. But I didn't bother to study, and by Christmas that year I had failed.

I was on a fast slide downward and I didn't know where it was taking me, nor did I really care. Every time I picked up a drink I was heading for a blackout, after which people told me what I had done during the lost time, but I had no recollection of the events they described. The blackouts really began to scare me. To this day I cannot remember the details of what I did for an entire two-year period of my life. However, I do remember that after I was asked to leave Confederation College in Thunder Bay, I lived off welfare and I continued to drink heavily while residing at the YMCA.

In 1961 my father remarried. He and his wife, Monica, who was from Pic River First Nation (about fifty miles from Mobert First Nation, my birthplace), were blessed with the birth of twins. Unfortunately, their daughter died at birth but their son survived. My stepmom and my dad named my stepbrother Donald Paul. Monica was very close to the family and Donald was a special little boy. He often reminds me of who my stepmom was, a strong courageous Ojibway woman who worked hard in our home. She exemplified kindness throughout her life. Monica passed away in September 1982.

It was during this same period that I met Sheila. She was staying on Mobert Reserve as preparation for an overseas mission with Canadian Lay Missioners. Sheila and I struck up a friendship and we talked endlessly about Indian issues, and incidentally about the direction of my life. She encouraged me to pursue my studies, to be part of the solution instead of part of the problem. Sheila decided to return to Alberta instead of going overseas and we continued to correspond by mail. During the summer of 1969 we decided to join an organization called Frontiers Foundation. They had a volunteer work program called Operation Beaver which sent young people into various northern communities to build homes and recreation centres. I was rather attracted to this idea and I greatly respected the man who ran the foundation. We spent the summer in Labrador constructing a recreation playground and campsite for the young kids there. That was a very eventful year.

Sheila and I married on 21 March 1970 and our son, Clem, was born on 8 September 1970. Sheila was teaching in Toronto and I attended Centennial College and completed my diploma in social services. Shortly afterward we moved to Peterborough and I went to Trent University and entered the native studies program. Though still drinking I managed, barely, to keep up my studies at university. Sheila always supported any life-affirming decisions I made. I never considered myself intelligent enough to finish any postsecondary educational program, but Sheila helped me to believe in myself. Her greatest gift to me was her encouragement and support.

We had our ups and downs, and I made life difficult for her. I never let her know when she could expect me home and my moods were extremely inconsistent. I was still drinking and very unpredictable. This created great anxiety and stress for her. Eventually it destroyed our marriage. I didn't know how to love her because I didn't love myself. Alana, our daughter, was born on 26 June 1975. Alana and her brother Clem are like gifts to life itself, bright well-balanced young people with wonderful personalities.

My problems were intensifying. I was draining Sheila's strength and it was then that we decided to split up and go our separate ways. Having nowhere to go I packed my suitcase and went down to the bus station in Peterborough. Once again I was faced with the now-familiar decision: should I go east or west? I pulled a coin out of my pocket and tossed it to the ground – "heads," I go east, "tails," I go west. When the coin landed "heads," I went east. I bought a ticket to Ottawa and got on the first bus. I had no plans. I felt unloved and lonely, but I had a burning desire to belong somewhere, or to someone.

I am forever grateful that my two children are gifted and enjoy good health. In my life's passage I have learned how and when to give thanks, I can honesty thank you, Great Spirit, for both my beautiful children.

The Middle Years

I wish the middle years had begun and remained on a straighter path. I begin this chapter of my life with the voice of my daughter Alana when she was sixteen.

The Destroyer

You think I am harmless
I have the power
I have the power to destroy
I can destroy your body
Maybe not all at once
Just maybe one part at a time
The choice is mine.

I have the power to destroy
I can destroy your brain
Maybe in a serious way
Or, maybe, just maybe, minor
The choice is mine.

I have the power to destroy
I can destroy your friendships
Maybe your nearest and dearest
Or, maybe, just maybe, not one of your best
The choice is mine.

I have the power to destroy
I can destroy your family
Maybe for the rest of your life
Or, maybe, just maybe for a short time
The choice is mine.

I am the Destroyer
Just give me the choice
And you'll be mine.

The Destroyer, by Alana Nabigon, c. 1991

After my marriage failed I felt an even deeper sense of self-rejection. I didn't like who I was or what I had become. Deep in my heart I knew I was doing wrong but I could not stop myself. The power of alcohol was a lot stronger than my will to resist a drink. At no point in my drinking career was I aware of the fact that it was the first drink that caused all my problems. I always blamed it on my fifth or sixth drink. Little did I realize that if I had stayed away from the first one, I would not have had a problem with the fifth or sixth.

In Ottawa I met Georges Sioui, a Native and a sovereign subject of the Great Huron Nation. Georges had mentioned that Carleton University had a recruitment program for Native people in the field of social work. I had nothing else to do so I considered his suggestion and applied to the program. I was accepted and enrolled in September 1975. My first semester at Carleton was very difficult because I didn't know the system, nor did I understand the proper way to write papers at the graduate level. Slowly, with plenty of encouragement and support from Georges, I began to gain confidence. My whole life now consisted of books, papers, and a weekly forty-ounce bottle of rye. I had no girlfriends or sex life to speak of because alcohol had burned the sexual drive from my body. I lived mainly in an abstract world filled with theories and models of social policy and counselling techniques. I still had not acquired the skills to express my emotions and I could not develop relationships under any circumstances.

I went to parties that were organized by the School of Social Work and made a complete fool of myself at those social gatherings. My professors and fellow students alike began to shy away from me. I desperately wanted to be accepted by my peers and my professors but I wasn't ready to change my ways in order to gain their acceptance. My drinking was pushing people away. When I was in a drunken state I became very angry and insulting and I antagonized people, saying nasty things. When I was sober, I felt extremely remorseful for my behaviour. Alcoholism is a very lonely disease. It not only cripples the mind and feelings but it sabotages any ability to associate with healthier people.

Maurice, one of my professors, was responsible for teaching family counselling and direct intervention techniques. One afternoon I arrived at one of his classes, drunk. I don't remember exactly what I said or did, but I remember falling off the chair and passing out on the floor. There was hysteria in the room because nobody knew how to handle this crisis. I'm sure many of my classmates felt pity or contempt for my behaviour. I had given them a hands-on lesson for their career choice. The problem was that they didn't know how to help me because I was not ready to help myself. I felt extreme remorse and shame after that incident, but not enough to stop drinking.

There were many times when I felt inferior to my classmates at Carleton because, unlike them, I had not completed my undergraduate degree. I tried to compensate for these feelings of inferiority by impressing the other students with my knowledge of Indian issues and the Indian culture. At the same time I felt really phony about the whole thing. Not only was I three sheets to the wind most of the time but I had never been taught about the Four Directions, which are strongly emphasized in First Nations culture. I felt inadequate in all areas. I felt stupid because I was not good enough at academics and I did not know enough about my culture to have a valid opinion. I now know that healthy self-acceptance only comes when we follow a true honest path and work hard to discipline ourselves in the knowledge and practice of that path.

My own ignorance and manipulation of other people's help during this time created tremendous inner conflict in my mind and spirit and the only way I knew how to handle it was to wash my feelings away with alcohol. Of course, the more I drank the worse my problems became.

I felt like I was slipping into an abyss of insanity and there was not a damn thing I could do about it. I did my best to act normal but every time I drank I became a crazy person. There seemed to be two people living inside my body. When I was sober I was fairly rational and reasonable like most other people living in our world, but when I drank I became this darker person. I became antisocial, unreasonable, angry, and full of resentment. All of these undesirable characteristics surfaced and I didn't have any control over them.

There didn't seem to be any way out of my dilemma. I wanted to die. I thought of committing suicide, but I didn't have the courage to kill myself. In addition to my antisocial behaviour, I was rapidly becoming paranoid. There is a joke the Natives love to tell about never going to football games because they believe the players talk about them in the huddles. This joke became the reality of any social gatherings I attended. I had become afraid of my sobriety. Sometimes even my own shadow scared me. A paranoid alcoholic is not the best person to have around as your friend. My life was a mess but I didn't have the strength to look at my own situation. Amazingly, in spite of all my problems, I felt it was easier to criticize and feel superior to others. I was confused and unaware that I was in the middle of chaos. Positive values were absent in my life. I didn't know what it was like to eat a good meal or to have a decent night's sleep.

In spite of my confusion and heavy drinking I continued with my studies. I wrote a joint thesis with my good friend George Simard, an investigation into the transitional life of

Cree students coming in from Northern Ontario to attend high school and postsecondary institutions in the Ottawa area. We were interested in alienation and how the transition from reserve to city life affected their studies and social behaviour. Ironically I did not personally understand the concept of alienation because I was disconnected myself. However, as we began to examine the problems of Indian students in Ottawa in a systematic way, we discovered that the older students experienced more behavioural problems than the younger ones. We attributed this to the fact that older Indian students tended to be more aware of what was happening in their environment, while the younger ones were testing their strength.

I thought compassionately of these students but I also felt frustrated because I could do nothing to help them out. I was certainly in no position to act as a leader because of my own weakness. I could explain the problems but I couldn't provide the solutions because I was a problem myself. The sense of frustration I felt is very difficult to describe. It was a little like pushing against a boulder: although you do everything in your power to move it, it does not budge.

My approach to solving the problem was to write a report with recommendations to the Department of Indian Affairs, recommendations that I expected would be quickly implemented. In my ignorance and lack of experience I convinced myself it would be that easy to apply a solution. I thought I could fight the battle and change the system on my own. Like my secret hero, the Lone Ranger, I wanted to fight the crime bureaucracy singlehandedly. I had a revelation that my inflated ego thought would make me a saviour for the Cree students. In reality, I couldn't even save my own life because of my addiction to alcohol. The Cree students had not asked me to be their saviour. No rational person would think of taking on a bureaucracy with six thousand employees and a billion-dollar budget all by himself. A rational person would likely have joined a pressure or lobby group to gather more support and generate a response to the needs of the students from the James Bay area. I was living in a fantasy world and I was completely irrational because of my drinking.

On the academic side I was able to do the research and writing, so I continued to pursue my degree and in my final semester I left for Confederation College, in Thunder Bay, to do my field placement. George Simard and I were asked to explore the possibility of writing a proposal to develop a hostel for homeless men. Most of these men were alcoholics who had broken dreams and very little hope. I met some of them while doing my research. Their broken dreams and their culture of the street mirrored my own life. It was a frightening realization for me, but I still did not know what to do about it. I wanted desperately to reach out for help but I didn't have the courage, and although I had finally begun to realize what was wrong, I was not ready to change my way of life.

I drank with these men while I was doing research for the proposal. I too had lived on skid row in Winnipeg for six or seven months, so I knew what it was like to live from handout to handout and to be rejected by ordinary people. It is an awful feeling to know that you have drunk yourself to a stage where you are incapable of looking after yourself, and to feel the repulsion and the contempt that people have for you when you are asking for charity so you can buy more wine. I have deep empathy for skid row alcoholics. I was one of them and they are a part of me. The memory of skid row is firmly planted in my mind. I know what it is like to be at the bottom of the current system.

My graduation from Carleton in May 1977 was uneventful. I didn't have any career goals nor did I have any immediate plans so I bought a couple of bottles of whiskey and caught a train from Thunder Bay to Toronto. While I was on the train I met an old drinking buddy whom I had known for years. Roy and I went on a drinking binge that continued for six weeks. When we had finished our binge I was sick, scared, and confused. What was I going to do with myself? How was I supposed to support myself? There didn't seem to be any immediate answers. Eventually, I went back to Ottawa and checked out the possibility of a job with the federal government. Finally, I landed a job with the Department of Indian Affairs and Northern Development (DIAND) as a policy analyst. This job involved looking at problems with wide-reaching implications and providing recommendations at a national level. I believed I had the power to change the direction of the department, when in reality, I soon discovered, I had a minimal amount of influence.

The Long Road Home

My job as a policy analyst meant a lot to me and I wanted to do the right thing, so I tried to slow my drinking down and restrict it to weekends only. I tried hard to muster all my strength and use my will power to put down the bottle but the power of alcohol eventually took over again. I slipped back into my old patterns, taking time off work, being unreliable, and generally producing low-quality work. There was little substance to much of the material I wrote and I found myself expressing emotion rather than fact.

For example, while writing up a housing policy, I had not gathered enough of the basic statistical information that I needed so my conclusions were extremely flimsy. My ability to analyze policies had been eroded by alcohol. Even after reading articles and old policies on housing I was unable to understand what they said. I had few powers of comprehension or concentration. There had been a time in my life when I could read articles and summarize their meaning almost instantly. Now, at this stage in my drinking career, I was beginning to realize that the alcohol was breaking down my mental processes and this really scared me.

My mind was no longer capable of logical thought and I became terribly afraid and defensive at work. I became offensive toward my fellow employees, undermining their suggestions and ideas. "You guys don't understand because you're not Indian. How will you ever write policies for Indians if you don't understand them as a people?" This was my favourite way of insulting my colleagues and boss. They tried their best to cope with me, to enable us to work together in the production of useful policy papers, but I kept telling them that they could never understand. The real reason I harassed them was to hide my own weakened reading and writing skills. My co-workers were all good people but I was afraid to admit the truth to myself, that I had let them down.

One of my fondest memories of this job was a trip I took to the West Coast with my boss, Richard. We were working on some background papers for services pertaining to the status of Indians living in urban centres. We made arrangements to meet with the Indian people who were providing these services for the Natives in Calgary and Vancouver. There I met an exceptional young Native man who was working on the streets. He was looking after alcoholics and drug addicts in the inner core of Vancouver. His job was to find beds and referral services for these people who were down and out. He was very critical of the department's insensitivity regarding social services that catered to Indians living off the reserves. I knew how he felt because of my own personal experiences living on skid row and trying to help others in Winnipeg and Toronto. Remember the Lone Ranger who rode a horse named Silver? Well, this brave man's dedication and service towards his people made him a true workhorse who was perhaps the only silver lining in the perpetual cloud hanging over his people. Unfortunately, none of us had the power to change the department's policy with regard to off-reserve Indians. All we could do was recommend, to our managers and the federal cabinet, what should be done.

On our way back from Vancouver we stopped off in Calgary. There the mood of Native people toward the department I represented was very hostile. Urban Native leaders were quick to point out the department's insensitivity toward the life-and-death situations of our people. Professors from the School of Social Work at the University of Calgary were also very hostile. I too felt angry because of the department's nonperformance in these areas. Once again, there was very little that I personally could do about it.

It was under these circumstances that I got my job as a policy analyst for the Department of Indian Affairs and Northern Development. There were public and political expectations that DIAND should have been able to improve the social and economic conditions of the Indian people. This would have led to a new relationship with the Indian bands, reflecting their suggestion that they unite under the 1982 Constitution Act. However, changes in corporate culture happen with great difficulty. Both DIAND and the majority of chiefs representing Indian bands across the country are very conservative about actual changes. This climate led to frustrations within our communities and within myself. When we returned to Ottawa I drank to forget about the problems of the Indian people in the cities. I clouded my feelings because I felt inadequate as a father, a male, an employee, and a human being. I didn't know what to do with myself and I had no idea how I could change.

I was still working as a policy analyst when I met Laura. She turned out to be a very special lady. She was a Native employed by the department as a summer student. We started to go out together but my drinking came between us almost immediately. I thought she was going to drop me, but she didn't. She encouraged me in my work and, unlike me, she didn't think my efforts were all in vain. She started to emphasize my good qualities. I never believed her because I was very suspicious of anybody telling me that I was an okay guy. Her words compelled me to wonder what she wanted from me. She really didn't want anything but my companionship. She told me that she liked me because I was a hard worker but that I drank too much. The "but" was too hard to take. I resented her telling me that I drank too much. I was so critical of people's behaviour that I found it almost impossible to see goodness in anyone. Laura and I went out together for a year before I decided to quit drinking. After all those years in the grip of alcoholism the consequences of my lifetime addiction were beginning to unfold.

One day Richard, my supervisor, gave me a choice. He said I had to stop drinking or I would be fired. He suggested that I join the twenty-eight-day program at Poundmaker's Lodge in Edmonton, Alberta. I decided to accept his suggestion. Perhaps it was because of the threat of being fired once again from my job, or maybe it was the emotional tie to the name Poundmaker, which was the middle name Sheila and I had given our son, Clem. Whatever the cause, going to this healing lodge was the turning point in my journey to sobriety.

Poundmaker's Lodge is a Native American drug and alcohol treatment centre that opened its doors in the mid-seventies. It is located in St Albert, a suburb of Edmonton. The treatment program is based on a twelve-step recovery program, commonly referred to as Alcoholics Anonymous (AA), combined with the Native American healing traditions. AA is used to bring down the walls of denial in individuals who cannot admit they have an alcohol or drug addiction problem. As I well know, substance abusers often experience denial and delusion, which prevents them from looking at themselves. The Native healing traditions are used to build self-esteem. Many people begin their inner journey at Poundmaker's Lodge. Eddy Bellerose, who later became my spiritual master and elder, took me into a sweatlodge and I learned how to heal my soul and build my inner fire. I was discharged from Poundmaker's Lodge in February 1979.

After I quit drinking, I expected things to go a little more smoothly and my life to be more peaceful. During all the years that I was drinking I felt I was in a tumultuous storm. This was supposed to be the end of the pain. I had been sober only a couple of months when I realized I still had a lot of internal conflict within me that I had not yet dealt with. Old and new anger welled up inside of me because I had never been taught how to handle or honour my own needs. I felt emotions twisting me, disturbing my vision of a new beginning, especially now that I was caring for Laura. I really didn't know how to relax and enjoy myself because I was too wrapped up in my own inner conflict. We went for long walks in the Kingston area, but they were not really relaxed, healing walks. I always wanted to debate and argue with her.

The answer was unexpected and appeared as a pebble dropping into the pond of my own recognition. Its simple rippling effect drew the attention of my conscious awareness. One day after one of these walks and talks with Laura I suddenly came to the realization that my constant emotional pain resulted from a path of self-inflicted agony that had come from not accepting responsibility for my own life. Simultaneously, I accepted that I could never expect anyone to look after me. Here I was, thirty-nine years old, behaving like a fourteen-year-old brat because I was in a relationship that I could not handle. I talked to Laura about my plans to change myself; about how I wanted to become a successful person and of course all the grand plans I envisioned to go along with it. I wanted to be a professional lawyer, social worker, and teacher all wrapped into one. Laura had encouraged me to do these things but wisely counselled me to be more patient. There was no need to rush into anything because I had all the time in the world. I didn't understand the word patience because I had so little of it. I never recognized the fact that until I had learned to tolerate myself, I could never tolerate another human being. Now I grasped what Laura was trying to teach me, to slow down and look after myself.

She had taught me the value of the Nnishnaabe, the Indian peoples' first given name, which means "Good Beings." A human-being, not a human-doing.

In August of 1979 I switched jobs within the department. I moved from the position of policy analyst to a position in Inter-Cultural Training. My responsibility was to reduce prejudice within the department itself. I was responsible for improving human relations between Indian and White people at work. I wondered how I could possibly do that when my own life was a mess and I had difficulty getting along with others. "Maybe they're giving me this job because I'm having such a hard time understanding the basic harmony of human beings," I reasoned.

Some Native Elders – Eddy Bellerose, Abe Burnstick, another senior Elder who wishes to remain anonymous, and their helper, Michael – came into my life at this time through a mutual friend Elders carry the ancient ways of our people. They are the Healers. By the time I met these generous people I was completely defeated by drinking. I was at a crossroads in my life. Eddy, my spiritual master, said, "You have a choice. You can either pickup your sacred bundle or you can die from drinking."

In order for me to carry my sacred bundle, I needed strength to walk the sacred path that the Creator had intended for me. Eddy suggested a four-day fast, without food or water, to begin my sacred journey. I had to learn how to live like the spirits, he said. Spirits have no need for food or water. If we acknowledge each other, we give each other strength, and this same principle applies in the spirit world. When we acknowledge the spirits, they in turn give us strength. Only then could I pick up the ancient teachings of my people. This is the courage I needed. My bundle's core is tobacco, sweetgrass, sage, cedar, the sacred pipe, and the sweatlodge. Fasting and ancient teachings from the Elders helped me set aside the alcohol and pick up and carry my sacred pipe.

I brought the Elders into the department to teach human relations through Native cultural beliefs. They came and used Native philosophy and Native psychology to improve human relations within our workplace. We received many good remarks about the quality of their workshops. Of course, some people expressed negative comments but that was to be expected. Not everybody agreed with the Elders' approach, but I was more than pleased. They were very good at their work and I really valued Richard's support of my choices.

Through time Richard taught me the value of making the bureaucratic system work toward my goals. I was pleased to have his support for my new-found role within the Department. We initiated the Elders' five-day workshop program in Edmonton, Yellowknife, Whitehorse, and Ottawa. Every Native nation was represented, in addition to people from other races as well. There was a general consensus within the workshops that Native values and Native concepts were very useful for developing good human relations.

I needed things to go well at this time. I had some strength, but I could not handle too much criticism or pressure. The Elders helped me deal with the pressure and conflict by being there and providing their support. They had their own firm called "Four Skies Consulting." I am forever grateful to these Elders with generous hearts. They played a very important part in my becoming sober and awakened me in a good way so that I could become a useful human being. I think the most valuable gift the Elders gave me was teaching me how to pray, something I had not done for years. This, I will never forget.

There Is No Middle Ground

There are many people who have seen the way things are,
And have asked almost in despair,
But what can I do?
And the only answer has been,
You have to do something about You.
Only you can decide whether you will be a part of
This destruction or whether you will set
Your heart and mind against it.
You may not be able to change where you work or how
You earn your living,
But you are totally responsible for the direction that
You give your own life.

We are only visitors here in this part of Creation,
We are guests of the one who owns this Creation.
We are always to keep in mind that we
Can own nothing here, not even our own lives.
So the purpose of life then, is
Not to acquire possessions
But to honour the Creator by how we live.

If we choose to be on the side of that great Positive Power
We have no choice but to set our hearts and minds
Against the destruction around us,
But thought without action is useless.
We must be on one side or the other
And how we will involve ourselves must be the free choice
    of everyone.

If we choose to act, we must act intelligently
And with common sense.
It means we will do everything in our power to understand
The questions that we choose to involve ourselves with.

But whatever we are, we must be action people
Even if the only action possible is to pray.

Power is given to each of us by the Creator.

They are on a journey, they have chosen their way.
They will restore their humanity.
They will take their place in the sun.
Will their path be a road of anger and bloodshed?
Or will it be a road they can walk on in honour and peace?

A new nation of people will be born again,
the sacred colour red will be restored
and no power on earth can prevent it.
You, that other colour of man,
can assist at the birth of this new nation,
Will you?

Reprinted from Arthur Soloman, *Songs for the People:
Teachings on the Natural Way*.
Edited by Michael Posluns, 67–8 (Toronto: NC Press, 1990).

A Meeting with
the Sweetgrass

Sweetgrass is found in the Prairie provinces, Quebec, and
the Maritimes. In addition it is found on Manitoulin
Island, and in other areas of Ontario. It may grow else-
where but for the most part it is concentrated in these
areas. Sweetgrass is Mother Earth's hair and when the
Elders weave the sweetgrass they braid it like you would
braid your own hair. When you burn a sweetgrass braid it
emits a pleasant, sweet-smelling odour. The Elders use the
smoke of the smouldering sweetgrass to cleanse the mind,
body, and spirit by smudging. Centring one's body is
equivalent to centring your intentions with the Spirit's
wishes. As human beings we were never meant to hold
physically on to our emotional anguish for as long as we
do. I had held onto my bitterness, my self-loathing, and
my addiction for too long. I now eagerly embraced the
sweetgrass. We always have a choice to participate in this
life but the decision is ours and only ours to make. When
the sweetgrass braid is used for spiritual purposes we
relieve our minds of past burdens, remain focused in the

present moment, and trust that the future path will unfold as it is meant to be revealed.

Once you have gone through the ritual of cleansing, sweetgrass comes to represent the simple kindness that we have as children of creation. All children have a simple way of being kind to each other. When I burn the sweetgrass, I use it to smudge my mind, body, and spirit. I am reminding myself of the simple virtues inherited in our nature. Good Beings, all beings, have the right to heal, that is our way. It is the internal wish of all human beings on the face of this Earth to find their aspirations, to heal and remain in the healing fire called "peace."

My ancestry, the old way, shares all teachings through stories that relate human experiences within Nature. The following story, or allegory, is my way of honouring my personal experience of healing and rebuilding my inner fire.

A long time ago a loon was badly hurt. His spirit was broken, and his mind and body were confused because he drank too much alcohol. This loon lived on the lake of fire-water and he was surrounded by many other loons who lived in the same state of confusion. The lake was polluted and the surroundings of the lake were not very pretty to look at because all the loons that lived on the lake drank too much. One day the loon met three other loons from a different lake. The confused loon, the one with the broken spirit, began to talk with the visiting loons. The two loons, Eddy and Michael, were generous and took time to communicate with the loon. They talked and walked the sweetgrass road with the broken-spirited loon. They told him that "only through simple honesty and kindness are we able to build our true fire. If we cannot build this fire we eventually die."

The loon imagined dying on this lake as a broken spirit who had never known love. The three loons assured him that "love embraces everything. Love does not exclude anything. If we cannot love ourselves," they told him, "then we can never experience the love of someone else." The loon's narrow vision caused him to wonder, "How can I love when there is so much cruelty and injustice?" He was engulfed in his feelings of self-pity, leaving little or no room for his healing. The loon didn't feel he had the strength to follow the sweetgrass road. He tried for many months but kept stumbling and falling down. The loon felt his wings could not lift him out of his despair.

One winter he met a fourth loon, who was called John. John showed the broken-spirited loon what the three other loons were trying to tell him. This wise old loon took him and showed him how to pray in the Native way. Together, the four strong loons, Eddy, Michael, Abe, and John, taught the loon with the broken spirit how to pray the Native way.

Gradually, the loon with the broken spirit began to feel his fire and he left the lake of confusion, pain, and violence. He didn't want any more water from this lake, the lake that was full of poison. The four strong loons carried the loon with the broken spirit on their backs and they flew through the sky until they found a quiet spot on the ground, and they taught him the old ways. The loon with the broken spirit slowly began to feel good about himself. He no longer desired a drink from the lake of poison. The compulsion of the past left him entirely. He didn't want to drink any more. He never wanted to touch that firewater again!

Habits of human beings, formed over decades, do not change quickly. Although I experienced, through reconnection with my Native traditional spiritual teachings, a change of heart that was in some ways euphoric, I still had my old patterns of acting and thinking. Shortly after I stopped drinking, I became aware of feelings I had not dealt with for years. Anger, guilt, and fear had controlled my behaviour. My mind was not strong enough to generate good thoughts and I could not create feelings such as joy and happiness without some part of me thinking, "This is too good to last." So, of course the goodness of peace was constantly under the threat of past patterns. I needed to practise the principles of honesty and kindness through sweetgrass on a daily basis. I wanted with all my heart to learn how to live harmoniously with the Spirit and other people. I had come full circle and now I had to deal with reality.

Corrupt, abrasive feelings about myself had surfaced and I realized that I could not handle the legacy of alcohol alone.

"You don't sober up and become a healthy person overnight," the Elders told me. "You took years to get where you are and it takes time to heal the damage you did to yourself. Alcohol is a poison and if you poison your body for many years it is going to affect you in many ways."

Alcohol's legacies began to surface everywhere. Having drunk myself into a state of paralysis for decades, I was now trying to get to know myself and feel comfortable within my body. For the first time, I took a complete and honest inventory of my life. I had lost my family because of drinking. I was not sober when I was studying and I am sure I missed a lot of relevant information. My tendency to blame others caused me to feel I had received an incomplete education. I had wrecked a third of my life. My recklessness left me with a scar I will have to contend with every waking moment. I lost my right arm because of alcohol. My ruthless habit of turning my guilt inward, the only pattern I knew from childhood, had to be broken. The toxic spell of anger and anguish had to be dealt with but I wasn't sure how to handle all this confusion.

"It's unthinkable," the Elders told me, "that a sick body will hold a healthy mind. It's logical that if you have a sick body you will have a sick mind."

I understood that simple statement. My mind was not very healthy when I sobered up, but I was able to take stock and do an inventory of my condition. The sweetgrass helped me empty out these feelings that had filled the hollowness in my chest. But what would I put in its place?

The Natural Cycle of Life

To contend with the painful feelings that were part of the healing process, the Elders gave me another indispensable spiritual tool called "the Hub." This gift of the Hub was, and still is, extremely useful to me. I use it on a daily basis to maintain balance in my life. The Hub can be applied at each and every stage of life. It helps me orient myself before I reach the point of despair. The Hub is basically a personality theory and it explains human behaviour and all its dynamics. Included within the Hub are the four stages of life, infancy, youth, adulthood, and Elder years. My new elixir has no magic in it, only practical solid information.

I believe the Creator gave all His children truth. My people's teachings are as old and as precious as all indigenous teachings globally. I read a study once that described children's development through art. Psychiatrists found that in every society and culture, no matter what the religion, the children were taught by the age of three, if there were no abnormalities in their mental capacities, how to draw a complete circle. By the age of six the children would begin colouring the circle yellow, and by the ages of eight to fourteen they instinctively drew four axes, or cardinal points, resembling rays of sunlight.

The teachings of the circle of life are simple in their terms but by no means simplistic in nature. Native people have always honoured the natural progression of human development and had rites of passage to reflect our internal beauty. At each point of growth the human being has a sense of progress as well as a dignified ritual through which we signify the transition from one stage of growth to the next.

The first rite of passage begins with a naming ceremony for the baby. Every community has an individual who is gifted in the giving of names. This person enters the Spirit World through his or her drum or pipe. The spirits in turn name the baby through the namegiver. I was given the name Little Loon by my maternal grandmother. So much has been taken from my people. I am happy to be one of the grateful First Nations people whose spirit name has been received in the oral tradition from my ancestor's mouth. My clan is also Loon. The Loon clans are the internal chiefs of their communities.

During the 1950s, many of our traditions were upheld as a natural extension of our daily habits. The adults taught the young the value of sharing and survival skills. Youths between the ages of twelve and fourteen (usually during puberty) were guided by the teachings of spiritual law. Males were left alone in the forest as their rite of passage. There they were given training and tools and expected to survive in the bush alone. Females were taken into ceremonies for their first Moontime (menstruation), as their rite of passage. Thus all youths experienced a period of recognition for their journey into adulthood. They were taught to be proud of their bodies and to respect all facets of their being. My own parents taught me all this by example because the actual teachings from the Elders, were suppressed in that day. Traditionally youths entering adulthood were also introduced to fasting as part of the way to understanding their place in the world and how things were interconnected. Fasting is also an introduction to the Spirit World. Native people were taught not to be afraid to speak about communicating with our ancestors, whom we identify as our allies. On one television show, for example, a young man practising shamanism had been contacted by the spirit of a Grandfather. He asked the spirit, "How come I can see you and the others can't?" The Grandfather answered, "That's because everyone else thinks I'm dead; you know better." This hints that the practice of contacting the Spirit World continues today.

Finally, some Elders, in the latter stages of life, through life's experience and spiritual ceremonies, are able to heal individuals and communities. We refer to the Elders as our masters and mentors because they mediate between us and the Spirit World. These four life stages and the Hub are interwoven into the Medicine Wheel: more specifically, infancy can be located in the East, youth in the South, adulthood in the West, and the Elder, who represents strength and wisdom, in the North.

I did not, of course, learn all these teachings in the initial phase of my recovery from addiction. As Eddy, my mentor, always said, "Have patience, Herb, the wisdom of our ancestors is rich and powerful, and right now you must have the humility to pray and learn slowly." I learned that the natural cycle of life is based upon Nature's will to form circles. A bird does not build a square nest, it migrates towards the forces that govern gravity and builds itself a circular bed. Try to imagine three circles, one inside the other (fig. 2). The outer circle represents the negative side of life. The middle circle represents the positive side, and the centre circle represents one's inner spiritual fire. The balance of these three parts is the ideal medium that one strives for in life. The circles are divided into four directions: North, South, East, and West, resembling the points of a compass. (Each of the directions has a significant meaning, which will be explained in greater detail in the next chapter.) All aspects of a person's life can be placed on the Hub, which thereby provides a means of understanding the human condition. The Hub can be used as a means to guide a person towards the balance of both negative and positive circumstances that occur within every life.

When I was drinking I had many negative emotions, most of them springing from the inadequacies that dominated my life's force. Feelings of inferiority appear on the outer circle, in the first section called the East. A person who feels inferior does not know that he or she is equal to the next person. I felt inferior to everybody. I had compensated for this feeling by acting superior to the people

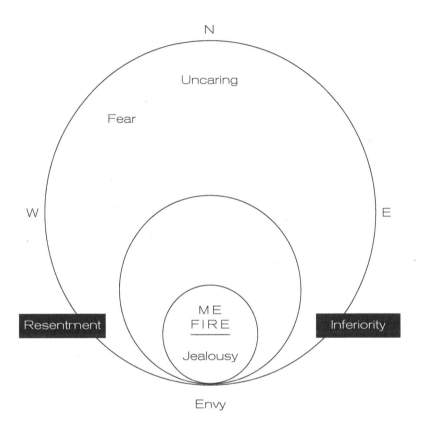

Fig. 2
The Hub

The eagle feather represents balance. The eagle uses its feathers to balance itself in flight.

The inner circle represents positive values, while the outer circle represents negative values. Native people who walk the red road attempt to balance their lives between goodness and fear.

around me. Usually I was able to maintain my act of superiority because I was better educated than the people that I associated with. This does not excuse my bad behaviour, but I want to be honest and explain the truth as I understand it.

The Elders explained that, "when a person feels inferior, he or she begins to envy other people." Envy is simply defined as wanting what other people have, but not being willing to do the work necessary to achieve it. I envied other people's happiness, success, status, and material wealth. However, I was not willing to work for these things. I was lazy, and envy controlled me. All I did was drink and fantasize. I had fantasies of being rich and handsome, with lots of girlfriends; of taking long holidays all over the world. The sad part about these fantasies is that I actually used to try to live them out. Somehow I was always shocked back into reality, which made me angrier. Escaping reality was my way of coping with stress but in doing so I was maintaining a falsehood.

An envious person usually harbours resentment. Resentment, which is represented in the West on the Hub, means re-feeling the negative feelings that had occurred in the past. I held many resentments after I had sobered up, including resentment of advice on how to correct my negative behaviour! My close friends sometimes pointed out my resentments and I didn't like what they had to say. It is very hard to receive the truth about yourself. I resented Richard for reprimanding me when I drank on the job. When I think about that today I realize that he probably saved my life. If he hadn't had the courage to say, "Herb, you drink too much," I would have continued to drink. He put pressure on me to stop drinking. I only valued my job because it provided me with food, clothing, and shelter. At that time I was not capable of any job satisfaction because I was too confused. I am now grateful to friends like Richard for having strict boundaries and limiting me to the choice of sobering up or being fired.

I resented the federal government for breaking its treaties and promises to the Native people, for stealing our land; and the Church for robbing us of our culture and our spirituality. While I was busy resenting the federal government for its misdeeds, it was I who felt hurt. I was the real loser. It takes a lot of energy to hold on to resentment. When your mind and feelings are focused on resentment your world is coloured with hatred. You cannot see much else. The consequence of resentment is narrow-mindedness. It is not a pleasant way to live, and most of all, you sacrifice your vision.

The attitude of uncaring is represented in the North. When I was drinking, I didn't care about my physical condition, my job, or my children. There were many things I didn't care about. More importantly, I didn't care about myself. Today, as I live a sober life, there are times when I don't care about things, but that feeling doesn't last very long. I am able to balance myself by remaining focused on myself and attending to my own needs and desires.

A person who feels inferior, envious, resentful, and uncaring usually harbours jealousies as well. Jealousy is represented as the negative side of the centre circle. A jealous person who cannot listen becomes very possessive. He or she thinks in terms of "my" children, "my" culture, "my" land, "my" life. Everything is mine, mine, mine. A jealous person doesn't know how to share. After I sobered up I came face to face with this jealousy.

My jealousies were of my land – the government had no right to steal "my" land. I classified all government people as swindlers and crooks. This is not necessarily so. There are a lot of good people in government. I pushed people away through my jealousy because I didn't know how to share and listen to my friends and other people around me. Jealousy puts out the fire of affection. A jealous person has no affection for themselves or others. I have now begun the process of peeling the outer layers of the negative side of life, a bit like peeling off the outer layers of an onion. I had to peel away the layers of fear to experience the goodness within me.

The fear in one's life is marked by the negative side of the North and appears as "not caring." The odds are stacked deeply against you when you are contending with an inferiority complex: you envy your fellow man; you resent that you do not have the material possessions that he has acquired; you are jealous because you do not know how to care enough about yourself to get help. The Elders taught me this is how a fearful person experiences life, and it is their opinion that most alcoholics are fearful people. They are controlled by the negative side of the Hub and they have no strength or know-how to work through fear. I testify in truth and support the Elders' opinion because I was a drunk, and I didn't have the strength to deal with fear when I was drinking.

The positive side of the Hub is the middle circle. Starting in the East again, a number of positive aspects are represented such as good feelings, food, and vision. To have a clear mind and feelings of well-being, one needs good food. Both physical and spiritual food are represented here. Appropriate sharing of feelings, not minimizing or exaggerating them, is relevant to healing. No matter what they are, it is very important to honour your emotions. When I choose not to share my feelings I begin to feel those old feelings of inferiority. There are many beneficial things associated with feeling good about yourself. Eating nutritious food and taking regular exercise are very important. Also, doing the best that I can at my job or in anything I am doing helps me feel good about myself. I find that feeling fine goes hand in hand with self-discipline, concern about others, and caring for myself. Today, I have no problem expressing my emotions. I can give and take within the proper boundaries. I thank the Great Spirit for this lesson.

A good feeling from within usually leads to good relationships with oneself and others. Relationships, time, and patience are represented in the South. It takes a long time to understand your feelings, especially after years of suppressing them. I believe that time and patience go together. These two elements are needed to have a rewarding relationship with the self. If we are always in a rush and never have time for ourselves or for others, it will not be long before we feel alienated. How impatient I was in my drinking days! I never had the time to listen to my own or another's feelings, nor did I have time to sit and be with another human being. Relationships with oneself and others require an inner quietness and an inner peace that is gained by listening. I have found this to be true over the years that I have been sober.

A friend of mine, Autumn Lee, who has been sober for many years, told me a story about time and feelings. I call Autumn Lee my "sober companion" because that is what she is, a very good companion. Her story has helped my in the understanding of the Sweetgrass Road, as the Elders call it. A carver takes a piece of marble, and each day he chips away at it. Days pass into months and after many months, the marble begins to take on form and beauty. Eventually, after much work, he completes a statue that has grace. I believe it is the same with sobriety. When I was first introduced to the Hub I was rough around the edges. My drinking years were marked by dishonesty and the lack of trust between others and myself. I didn't even know the meaning of the word trust, so I didn't know who I was except that I was angry and at times depressed. With the Hub and the burning of the sweetgrass, I could remind myself to follow the teachings and slowly I began to heal myself. Like the carver and the statue, I was able to take on a new form of life. The Hub teaches me about my inner grace and beauty. These teachings have replaced the hollowness in my chest. My internal void has been filled with the essence of my unique self. I feel it is a kind of grace. My understanding of grace is inner quietness and calm.

Moving on to the West, if I develop a good relationship with myself and others, I will eventually learn how to respect myself and all people. The literal meaning of respect is to look twice. If I look twice at myself, I realize I am a good person. We do not have to be extraordinary people. Most human beings, like myself, are somewhere in between the forces that govern sainthood and evil. The negative aspect of life is in place, in the outer circle of the Hub, so we may learn to harness its teachings and grow to serve the positive all the more.

The strongest example I can find in Nature comes from Sister Water, the cradle of Mother Earth's womb. In her depth can be found the teachings of the oyster totem. Here the oyster's precious jewel, a pearl that starts out as a grain of sand, is nothing more than an irritant that has entered the barnacle or oyster at some point and cannot be removed. That oyster has lodged in its folds something that is very painful to its habitat-being. The sand cannot be removed and now the oyster must contend with it, using its natural abilities to deal with the situation. Unlike humans who pretend "it" will go away, the clam pulls from its inner qualities a working solution. The clam totem's teaching resembles our own feeble attempts to make peace with our emotions. It didn't ask for the lesson, but it was forced to take a negative aspect of life and work with its principles. In this instance Nature teaches the oyster to tap into its intrinsic abilities to protect itself from corrosion. The oyster now heaves up its own mucus in multiple layers until it polishes smooth the intrusive entity – the grain of sand. Time then becomes the key. The outcome is a jewel that is admired by all.

If we do not honour the negative side of life we as humans either fall very ill or, worse, inflict our pain upon each other. Touching the negative aspects of life can be beneficial. If we learn to honour and recognize all of our emotions, including the negative qualities, we can and will become the bearers of our own pearls of wisdom.

I'm glad I have some fears within me because it is only through dealing with my human weaknesses of inferiority, envy, resentment, not caring, and jealousy, known as the "five little rascals," that I can learn and grow. Ironically it is through my weaknesses that I have learned to teach myself to be strong. I can be honest and kind with myself. Before I point my finger and blame, accuse, or gossip about another, I should point my finger towards myself and look at my own behaviour. My mind, eyes, ears, and mouth can teach me how to be a good person by using the Hub. Thinking about what the words on the Hub mean and being honest and kind with myself helps me to live the traditional Native way.

Since I started to use the sweetgrass, I have learned how to feel, to relate, to respect myself, and to care. Because I live the opposite of the five little rascals, I have learned how to build my inner spiritual fire. The hub of my being is now the light of my fire. I call it fire because when I think of fire, I think of the sweetgrass ceremony and a feeling of warmth and feelings of beauty engulf my senses. Only through the help of the Elders was I able to build my fire. I use my fire to protect myself from fear. The fire acts as a shield. I feel I never have to drink again but I must continue to ask for help. I need to ask the Great Spirit for help and I need to be honest and try to change my fear. There are always the five rascals to contend with in life – we should never discount their strength. I can do this by redirecting, or rechannelling, the fear energy into goodness.

I still struggle to remind myself of self-honesty and self-kindness in order to achieve balance. I believe that there is no such thing as perfection. People can grow if they have the strength to be honest within themselves.

The One You Feed

An old Ojibway Elder was
Teaching his grandchildren about life.
He said to them, "A fight is going on inside
Me ... it is a terrible fight and it is between two
Martens.

"One Marten represents fear, envy, resentment,
Inferiority, uncaring and jealousy.

"The other Marten stands for wisdom, love, respect,
Truth, honesty, humility, bravery
And faith.

"This same fight is going on inside you, and
Inside every other person, too."

They thought about it for a minute and then one
Child asked his grandfather,
"Which Marten will win?"
The old Ojibway Elder simply replied ...
"The one you feed."

Author unknown

Spirit Road

"Go Back!" Go back and listen
To the truth of your ancient teachings
They are the voice of the Creator guiding you

"Go Back!" Go back and look –
See! The Spirit Road is bright
It radiates the sacred colours
Of the four directions, all the nations.
My people, your people,
The Red and Yellow, the Black and White,
See! All our relations together on the Spirit Road.

Follow! Follow this road out of the canyons of despair,
Over the steep cliffs of pain and rejection.
That road's light is always enough,
Even for only one step at a time.

"Go Back!" Go back and walk,
Walk with firmness and care,
Stay close to your hearts light.
Learn all that the Creator teaches, hold it close to your heart.
Know that on this Spirit Road you are never alone.

Know that you are loved and that you walk in love
On the Spirit Road.

Annie Elizabeth Wenger

The Four Sacred Directions

In our Native culture, we relate to and learn much by observing Nature. Two paths are available to us. One is a dark and anxious way. Those who exclusively or persistently follow it see the Earth only as a resource to be exploited. Their guide is gold, or the hope of receiving monetary rewards. On this path their nurturing Mother will become the dark Mother and destroy them. The other option is the Medicine Wheel path. The spiritual interpretation of the Native world view is divided into the Four Sacred Directions (see fig. 3). These directions are used to search for harmony and peace from within. All those who embark upon this path hold the land in trust. Their every act is of leadership and their every service is directed towards Mother Earth, Sky Nation, or Spirit World and all living creatures in between that sustain our lives. These two forces are intertwined, creating both a way of joy and sadness that is inseparable from the human condition.

As with a great deal of other ancient wisdom, the Medicine Wheel has no written record. It has remained a part of the daily rituals and ceremonies dating as far back as the

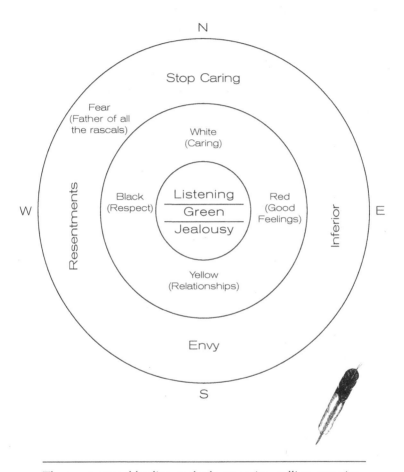

Fig. 3
The Medicine Wheel

N

Stop Caring

Fear
(Father of all
the rascals)

White
(Caring)

W

Resentments

Black
(Respect)

Listening

Green

Jealousy

Red
(Good
Feelings)

Inferior

E

Yellow
(Relationships)

Envy

S

The seven natural healing methods are crying, yelling, sweating, yawning, talking, laughing, and shaking. The eagle feather represents balance between positive and negative, reflecting the way the eagle uses its feathers to balance and direct its flight.

early Stone Age and is now being revealed by its keepers, the indigenous peoples. The wisdom is always presented as a circle, or in the shape of a wheel. Mastering the knowledge attached to it requires a lifetime of effort, learning, and practice. Although its four paths are always followed in a clockwise direction, one may start growing anywhere on the Medicine Wheel. If one follows the teachings of the Medicine Wheel, one will always find healing in the Four Directions, or four aspects of the self – spiritual, emotional, physical, and mental.

Each of the four cardinal directions of the Wheel has specific powers and gifts, which are taught by a spiritual teacher. In addition, each direction has been assigned a specific meaning and colours that have a special teaching.

According to the legend as told by our Elders, the four races (red, yellow, black, and white) of humankind lived on a huge piece of land. Then the snow on top of the mountains (known as Wabigoon in Ojibway) melted. This was also known as the ice age. The land was divided and we all lived together on North and South America. This division of land became known as the five continents.

The East Door

It is believed that the Creator began life in the East, symbolized by the colour red. In the spring, when the east wind blows a soft breeze, the Earth, our Mother, begins to get warmer as the sun warms her. If you notice plants, especially the roots and the alder shoots, they turn a reddish brown. Spring is symbolized by the colour red because the roots are renewing themselves just as the Earth renews herself. The Earth cleanses herself every spring just as a woman's womb is cleansed once a month. Spring is a healing season wherein all life is reborn. New life and new feelings come to all living things in the spring season.

Aboriginal people are represented in the East, and the Creator bestowed the gifts of food, feelings, and vision on these people. The Turtle clan and the Fish clan are also represented in the East. Traditionally, these clans were poets and sacred orators. The medicine of tobacco was presented to the Nnishnaabe by the Creator. Tobacco is used as an offering in all our ceremonies. In the spring the animals have their young and we use those animals for food. In the Ojibway culture the symbols for food are the moose and whitefish. Historically the moose provided us with clothing, tools from the bone, meat, and snowshoes among other things. The four-legged ones and fish were great providers of sustenance. I am grateful for the animal spirits because they are lifegivers. If we continue to abuse our interdependence with the food chain our lives will be made very difficult. We are responsible for the quality of sustenance for the next seven generations. Food is medicine; it doctors and it heals us. In some of our farming practices we do not respect our limited resources. Without good-quality food we would not live very long.

The Four Sacred Directions help me to balance myself and to know my place in the world. The importance of a balanced diet cannot be overemphasized. I think of food as a sacred gift today. I don't take it for granted as I did during my years of drinking. Food is a lifegiver and we still don't understand how physical food transforms into the essence of the life force that gives us energy. I did not eat a balanced diet before. Sometimes I didn't eat for days. The lack of proper nutrition affected my physical and spiritual health. My mind and feelings suffered because of the lack of proper nutrition. Today, I am very careful with my diet. I eat meals of protein and greens and try to stay away from too much starch, like bread and spaghetti. I try to reduce my carbohydrate intake and increase my protein intake. Good food helps me with my feelings. I know that if I am hungry or if I overeat, I don't feel very good. Overindulgence contributes to negative thinking, or feeling guilty that I overate. I may get angry because my clothes become too tight if I overeat. Food does affect my feelings and if I eat good food, I am able to function a lot better and think more clearly.

In contrast to good feelings, feelings of inferiority also come from the East, the subconscious belief in one's inferiority to others. When this occurs many people become timid, or, conversely, they overcompensate with aggressive behaviour. Displaced aggression comes from an unbalanced East Door and can be traced directly to our homes. Our society now correctly labels it domestic violence. A perpetrator who raises his hand to beat his wife shows signs of inappropriately expressed anger. If you are feeling inferior you tend to pick on the weaker people around you and they are usually your wife and children. As you strengthen your sense of self-worth you usually stop these violent behaviours.

Traditional teachings from this direction bring a message of peace and harmony into our communities. The mother was and is today the primary teacher of our spiritual fire. She instructs her children on how to live a balanced life. In traditional times women held authority in the political, social, and economic spheres of family life. Women were honoured and respected by their men. This respect permeated throughout the community. Our collective responsibility today is to restore that respect.

I have a quiet inner confidence today and I value this because I never had it before. Previously, I didn't know what inner confidence meant, nor was I interested in finding out because of my sick, demented mind. Alcohol took me very far down the road to oblivion. It was not until I sobered up that I realized what kind of person I had become. I was not who I wanted to be. The harsh realization of who I was makes me more grateful today.

The South Door

The colour yellow is a symbol of summer, time, relationships, and the sun. At midday, the sun is facing south. The heat of summertime teaches us patience because it is too hot to move fast.

The G'-noo (Golden Eagle) is represented in the South. The Eagle is considered a very sacred bird by our people. We believe that the Eagle, being the creature that can fly the highest of all birds delivers our thoughts and prayers to the Creator. An Eagle's feather is held in great respect because it represents the highest virtues of our truth. The holder of an Eagle feather values a balanced life.

When I sit quietly with my Eagle feather I become aware of my feelings, thoughts, and spiritual ways. It is then that I talk to my Creator. This virtue helps me in my relationships with others and with myself. Silence can speak volumes. It has taught me to become aware of my mind, body, and spirit and rise above my daily problems.

When I went back to Mobert my grandparents helped me work through some old issues. I left Mobert as a young man because I resented being an Indian. I associated Indians with alcohol and laziness, which is how I began to see myself. I never recognized the strength of my grandparents twenty years ago. Mishomis and Nookemis lived a traditional life. Their marriage lasted for sixty-five years. They lived off the land, hunting and fishing, close to the animal kingdom and Nature. They taught by example. Today, fortunately, I recognize that my grandfather's gift of silence. His awareness of life and his forceful presence taught me a new approach when dealing with old anger and old resentment. At the same time it was my maternal grandmother who invited me back to the reserve. She recognized I had some skills that would benefit the community. I tried to share my knowledge and offer a little wisdom so that the children in the classroom might be able to use it now and in the future. I tried to be an example and I earnestly tried to be part of the solution, not the problem.

This was a mind-boggling and life-altering experience for me. At one time I was part of the destitute. Now my personal history was being used for resolution. We are helped to understand the self through our relationships with family, extended family, friends, and community. It takes time to understand our identity as human beings. We learn and understand the self by interacting with peers. Values are transmitted through our parents and institutions such as schools and churches. But we should also always try to associate with people who are leading a good life, to be part of a circle that is life-affirming.

The South also represents youth, the second stage of life. Puberty is a time of change for all young people. Adolescence is often a time of crisis. For young Natives, it is a time to define their position in their culture. The process of defining cultural heritage takes precedence over all other activities, including education. It is during this period of self-exploration that a young person's academic grades may begin to decline. Educators and parents forget to take this into consideration when there is a crisis at school. Elders and traditional teachers can help adolescents to understand and defuse the crisis.

Many things had changed in Mobert during the twenty years I was away. I did not know any of the young people. I only knew the people of my generation and the older ones. Today, I understand I am only a part of the cycle. I am the compost whose experiences will be used to cultivate healthy gardens. I am useful. Indians are born every day and Indians die every day and I am a part of the learning cycle within our race. I am just one flash in the pan, resembling the finite breath of the moose in wintertime. That thought humbles me. My ego has been cut down to size because I understand and accept my significance within the wheel that governs life.

Late in the summer the leaves start to turn yellow. Yellow reminds me of patience, which is essential to any relationship. Yellow people are represented in the South. Their teachings bring the gifts of time, patience, and relationships, because these are so highly valued in their culture. The opposite of a good relationship is envy. As I said earlier, envy can be defined as wanting what someone else has but not being willing to work for it. If envy is not dealt with in our sacred healing circles many of the little ones will react to and perpetuate our inherited pain and be forced to take the long road home. I call on all my brothers and sisters to begin expressing their pain. It is time to heal our relationships with ourselves.

The West Door

The colour black is a symbol of respect. It teaches us to look within and use the medicines (i.e./ tobacco, sweetgrass, and sage give us the strength to change the negative to positive). The quality of our inner life is enhanced when we understand and implement the word "respect." When the west wind comes, fall is around the corner. In the autumn all the plant life dies. The leaves on the trees and plants in our garden begin to change to the colour black. The leaves and plants begin to alter. Black in the fall also reminds me of the black people. The black people have experienced humility. In our way humility is understanding our sacred place within creation. They have taken more than their share from the cup of suffering. Humility is the recognition of our place within Nature. We have much to learn from the black people about respect.

I am mortal. You are mortal. Death is inevitable. The West door, that of the sacred buffalo, is the ancestor's path home. Every effort we put into leading a decent life will speak on our behalf when we stand before the Great Spirit as our lives are reviewed. I believe it is the living we must get right, not the dying. My grandparents are a wonderful example to me. My grandfather died at ninety-six years of age. When he was alive, he hunted, fished, and trapped wild animals. He lived intimately with Nature. He also had a strong spiritual life in the Christian tradition. I believe he lived as long as he did because he was able to take care of his mind, body, and spirit by being honest and kind. My grandmother was the same way. She was seventy-eight years old and she still followed my grandfather into the bush every fall to trap and hunt. She also lived a very traditional lifestyle, and she was close to Nature. Grandmother passed into the Spirit World in the summer of 1987.

I believe the key to my grandparents' contented and spiritual life was their ability to know their place within Nature and to practise the principles of honesty and kindness towards themselves and others. I feel humbled by their wisdom and their spiritual strength. Our Elders lead by example, by living a balanced life. No fame or notoriety is required. Only the strength and goodness to work for others in a selfless way. Living an honest life is a spiritual reward in itself.

If I think twice before making a decision or taking some action, my reasoning is good. When I was drinking there were many times when I did not think about anything. I just went ahead and did it because the attraction of alcohol was so strong. I had no reasoning power. Today, because of the water in my system my reasoning has improved. Our bodies are two-thirds water. Tears are the body's natural response to the healing of uncontrollable traumas.

Many adolescents have a difficult time reviewing their inner life because of change and crisis. Native spiritual leaders who have an intimate understanding of adolescence and healing ceremonies are accessible. There are times when dysfunctional families overburden their older children with the responsibility of taking care of younger siblings. This practice creates inner hostility and resentment. These feelings of resentment destroy any self-respect we may have. Elders and traditional teachers conduct sacred ceremonies to defuse resentment.

Water is a very important source of energy for me. I never really thought about it when I was drinking. I use water to cleanse myself both internally and externally. Our sister water is alive. But women, who are keepers of the water, tell me that her strength is depleting at an alarming rate. Like everything in life, you can have too much of a good thing. You can bloat yourself up. If you mix water and barley, you can make firewater and that could kill you too. Do not abuse the precious commodity of water. If you had to lug it from a dwindling well you would think twice about how and when we use her precious life force.

The North Door

White is a symbol of winter, movement, air, and caring. Caring can be defined by our level of interaction, within family, school, community, and nation. Isolation usually indicates that problems exist and they need to be dealt with accordingly. When the strong north wind blows everything turns white and we have the season of winter. The north wind is a great mover. It is a master of movement. It can move trees, houses, almost anything that gets in its way. This is a reminder that every action has a consequence, a caring one or one that promotes fear. Everyone therefore makes a difference either in a caring way or an uncaring way.

The Bear represents strength and healing. The Bear also hibernates every winter and we believe that she is fasting and praying for peace and harmony among the four colours of man. She is the protector of all First Nations ceremonies. White symbolizes the Caucasian race, which has led the world in technological achievements, but which in many cases continues to damage the environment, for example the ozone layer. We need collectively to heal the earth. I am a human being, therefore I use common sense. I like to think that way about all my brothers and sisters of the white, red, yellow, and black races.

We can pull together and use common sense to do the right thing, for ourselves and our children. I honestly believe that the goodness in people will overcome the inner fear, and that this fear will no longer control us. Common sense tells us that we have to work through this fear together. Today, I try to resist any racist attitudes because I know that every person has a gift to offer. We have commonalities; we all need clean air, food, sun, and water for our existence, we are interdependent. The sun does not only shine for Indians, it shines for everybody.

The importance of good clean air is vital to our mental, physical, and spiritual well-being. I remember several occasions during my drinking years when I drank in a basement in Toronto for days on end. I noticed, after some time, how stuffy the air was and how difficult it was to breathe. My hangovers and the stale air contributed to my slow suicide. Living in the city, I drifted away from thinking about Nature. I was concerned with survival, but most of all I was concerned with how I was going to get my next drink.

After I sat down and reviewed my life, I wrote down the gifts that the Creator provided for me. It was a revelation to me and I felt good because I accepted how vulnerable and weak I am without life givers (water, food, air, sun, fire). I used to get into deep philosophical debates in barrooms about questions such as "What is life?" Of course these discussions never got anywhere.

Life for me now is very simple. All forms of life require nourishment, the life givers. It is as simple as that. I no longer concern myself about the differences between spiritual beliefs and religions. I keep my spiritual beliefs simple and live them. I acknowledge the power of the sun, the water, the air, and food.

The statement "All human beings use common sense" is one that I believe I heard from my grandmother a long time ago. For her it was common sense to care. Care is as necessary as the air we breathe. Infants die if they are not cared for. If we are not taught to care for ourselves we will always be dependent, compulsively needing others to nurture us, which often leads to codependency in our relationships. Our belief is that caring is given to us in the North, around the sacred Hub. Caring affects our behaviour in every facet of our life. When I was drinking, my caring was reduced to a very low level. My movement was erratic and I had no direction. Some methods of natural healing through movement within are yelling, laughing, sweating, crying, yawning, and shaking. These can help a person overcome fear.

The Centre of All Things

It is understood that if you grasp the concept of guiding your life from the Four Sacred Directions, then you are operating form the centre of your being. Green is a healing colour, the symbolic colour of Mother Earth, which is at the centre of all things. Green also represents your fire and is symbolic of the creator living inside of us. The Earth nurtures the four colours of humankind and all living things. Thus, green and Mother Earth are in the centre circle on the Medicine Wheel. Also in the centre is ME. ME is the acronym for Mother Earth. ME is the site of my inner spiritual fire. When I am in balance with myself and all things, then I am in touch with my inner spiritual fire. Green is also a symbol of balance and listening. Spiritual leaders emphasize that we should listen and pay attention to the dark side of life so that we can learn and heal. The dark side can be defined by the five little rascals mentioned earlier. The dark side of green means we stop listening. The first step towards healing is to learn how to listen to the dark side. Listening helps us to make the appropriate changes from negative to positive behaviour.

A long time ago, my grandmother told me that the Earth is our garden. The Creator made this garden for us and it was up to us to live in harmony within our garden. When we take from Mother Earth to feed ourselves, we should always thank Mother Earth and the animals and put something back. The principle "Whenever you take, you must also give" was what my grandmother taught me.

Grandfather, a trapper, never wasted anything that he killed. He used everything for his livelihood. He had the greatest respect for all four-legged creatures. My father lived by this same belief. Through his way of living, he taught me the value of respect for Nature, although I never paid attention to his teaching for many, many years. I am glad my grandfather and my father taught me the value of respecting Nature.

The white race has improved technology for harvesting food from Nature, which makes life easier for us. But we should always remember that without Nature, human beings are nothing. Our dependency upon Nature should never be forgotten. I try not to forget about the lifegivers today. Nature's diversity, different colours, the smells of Nature, the sound of animals are very good things. They remind me of my dependency on Nature. They also remind me of the gifts that the Creator has provided for me to live on this Earth.

The sun is the hub of the universe. All of our planets in the solar system revolve around the sun. Without the sun the Earth would die. When I was drinking, I never really thought about this kind of thing. My mind was so closed and my vision so narrow that I did not take the time to appreciate what a gift the sun is until I met the Elders. As far as I was concerned, there was a sunrise and a sunset every day and that was it. The sun is the source of energy for my life. I also remember that the sun can burn me and destroy me. Like everything else, there has to be a balance. Overexposure to the sun or a lack of it will destroy me.

When the sun gets hot in August, I feel the presence and power of the Great Spirit. When the cold north wind blows in the winter, I can feel the presence and power of the Great Spirit. When I see how we harvest food through hunting and fishing, and when I see farms in the South, I can feel the power and the presence of the Great Spirit. For me it does not matter what you call her. You can call her God, or the Great Spirit, or Jesus. I believe there is only one supreme being that created Nature and human beings.

People have different ways and different methods of talking with the Creator, but behind all the different religions, including Native spirituality, it all means the same thing. It means learning to love ourselves and, through that love, growing and, thanking our Creator for our lives. I no longer bother debating about these things. I keep it simple.

The Struggle for
Spiritual Strength

The simplest of tasks can become overwhelming in a life
that is complicated. As Native people we of the First
Nations respect the simple manner in which the teachings
are handed down from our Elders. For thousands of years
the Elders, through our oral tradition, kept these teachings
alive so that I and others might live in harmony. The jewel
of our hearts can be polished in many ways, but it is getting to our healing that is vital.

My rites of passage did not come in a sequential order.
I had been given a spiritual name at birth and entered the
bush with my father at an early age, but my complicated
youth prevented me from entering adulthood with a vision
quest, a direction. In my adult life the sweetgrass, the Hub,
and the Four Sacred Directions were passed on to me by
the Elders, and now it was time that I began to apply these
teachings to my life. Fasting is a purification ritual as is a
vision quest, which facilitates one's spiritual growth process. It is very sacred within the context of the Nnishnaabe
culture. Fasting is known as an introduction to the Spirit

World where one may ask for and receive many blessings, or guiding imagery, for the entirety of one's life. In order to heal the fractured parts of myself, the Elders asked that I quest all Four Sacred Directions. That meant that I had to enter the bush on four separate occasions, without food or water. I won't lie to you, suffering is part of the healing.

The First Fast

During my first year of sobriety, I was invited by the Elders to go into the mountains, near Calgary. Healing cannot easily be achieved in the city. There is too much distraction there, the opposite of what we are trying to achieve. We went straight into the mountains with some friends and prayed in the traditional Native way. That meant that we had to abstain from eating and drinking water while living in the forest for four days and nights. This was done to signal our bodies' earnest attempt to make contact with the World of Spirit.

Questing for spiritual guidance initiated the cycle of my own spiritual renewal. Usually one starts with the East Door, the place of all beginnings. It was a great surprise and honour for me to have the Bear visit me during the first of a series of four fasts. The Bear is the ultimate healer and he had signalled to me that Bear is my spirit guide for life. Since that day he has protected every ceremony I carry out. When he appeared I felt his physical presence. The rough pads of his paws lay on my face and his warm breath heaved in my ear. It startled me because his presence was so real. This was a significant message from Spirit so I started my series of fasts with the North Door where the Bear Spirit resides. I prayed for honest and simple caring while I was on that fast. But caring was very hard for me to establish because for many years I had not cared. This fast was my first attempt to balance my life; to balance my life like Nature balances itself through the four changing seasons.

Red, the colour of the East Door, signifies renewal in the Aboriginal culture. Animals are one of our life supporters. The turtle spirit from the East heals and mends broken hearts and feelings. Each spring the animals multiply their numbers, regenerating our food supply. Fasting is our way of honouring their existence. Just as life begins in the East, we experience a time of renewal during the fast. Water is a symbol of the West Door. Two-thirds or more of our body consists of water. This shows us our connections to the lakes. The spirits don't require water or food and during the fast we can become more conscious of our spirituality by living without food and water. When we honour the spirits in this way, they honour us by giving us the power of understanding.

No dramatic change happened on my first fast, but I felt that the dark ugliness inside me had been cleansed a little and a small pilot light was beginning to flicker. It symbolized my struggle towards freedom and liberation from my fears. All my life fear had dominated me and the fast was a means for me to deal with my fear. I didn't realize it at the time but I was getting close to Mother Earth by denying myself sustenance for four days. I wanted desperately to open up and receive the grace of the Great Spirit by admitting I was a fearful person. I prayed for strength to build my fire and to become strong so that I might become a useful person again. I had experienced a little warmth and this felt good. It had been so long since I had felt warm-hearted.

When the four days were over, I felt that I had accomplished something worthwhile. It seems that anything worthwhile you do requires some sacrifice and hard work. The Elders mentioned that "there is no magic to praying the Native way, but it requires a lot of hard work and striving on your part." I wanted to change so badly that I was ready to put all my effort into the struggle towards balance in my life. I knew I was ready for a change and I wanted to cleanse away all of the negative feelings I had inside. I trusted the Elders unconditionally with my life. They were good teachers and, to this day, they are my best friends.

The Second Fast

My second fast took place in the Gatineau hills to the north of Ottawa during my second year of sobriety, in 1980. I had always felt alone, inferior, and unequal to the people around me. I had never felt that I belonged anywhere. So on my second fast, I fasted for good feelings. Feelings are symbolized at the East Door. I was always afraid to be alone in the bush, almost to the point of paranoia. My complex is a very common phenomenon. I always had the feeling there was something behind me. To deal with this fear I went into the bush and fasted for four days and four nights on my own.

Anything worthwhile takes time and the slow process of rehabilitation is no exception. As a child, I had simple faith and I wanted to recapture its essence through fasting; I was aiming for continuity and chose again to fast for my honesty and kind caring. While fasting alone, with a lot of time to think about my life, I reflected on the harm that I had caused myself and others. Being close to Nature during the fast helped me to be honest about the things I had done. I pondered over my vulnerability, weak and alone I was in Nature. Sensing that I was part of Creation helped reduce my big ego and I realized I was nothing without the help of Nature and the Great Spirit. I felt very humble because I knew then where my strength came from.

I felt weak and vulnerable during my second fast. Laura provided me with support during those gruelling days of solitude. She came to see me every day to find out if I was all right. Laura had a sore knee and it was a struggle for her to walk up the steep hill to where my lodge was, but she managed the climb. Despite her sore legs she came up the hill every day and I did not have any appreciation for what she was doing for me. I was engulfed in my anger and I had little time for gratitude. I had several visualizations as I mentally attempted to cleanse myself; to rid myself of all the rage. I tried to feed my anger to the sacred fire but the anger lingered despite my efforts. On the fourth day of the fast, Laura informed me that my dad had become very ill. I knew he was ready to drop his robes and join the Spirit World only I didn't want to hear it at that time.

When I came out of the four-day fast relief flooded my body, but I had not experienced any spiritual revelations. I was very critical of myself and felt that my efforts had not been good enough. I was expecting magic, but there was no magic. I was furious with Laura. I know her intentions were honourable, but telling me about my dad on a retreat defeated the purpose of my isolation, or so I reasoned in my egoistic self-absorption. After that fast I said some harsh words to her and later I felt remorse for what I had said, but the damage was done. My father died on the last day of my fast. The same feeling of emptiness I had when my mother died resurfaced and for a while I felt so desperate that all I wanted to do was go back to drinking. I have since made peace with that feeling by taking care of my responsibilities in life.

The Great Spirit, through His wisdom, forces us to revisit our painful experiences in life. I believe He does this so we may learn and benefit from each and every one. This is a very difficult lesson and He taught it to me during my second fast, but it was not until much later that I came to understand its significance. For until we are able to experience painful memories without pain, we have not accomplished the knowledge and wisdom of its teaching.

The Third Fast

On my third fast, my friend Georges Sioui came with me. This time I fasted for my relationship with myself. The hub of my being still seemed somewhat of a mystery to me but at least I was seeking answers. Georges was a wonderful healing agent because we shared our feelings with each other. We remained in the bush for three days. We made a sacred fire which we fed continuously; we talked and made our sacrifice together. I was very strong in my desire to get close to my inner self and get near to the spirits. After the fast was over, I felt clean inside and I felt good about my condition of healing. My mind was getting a little clearer, but the plateau I was aiming for was still out of reach.

In the dark corners of my mind, I was looking for a quick fix. I wanted to be blessed with a visit from the Great Spirit, and although I prayed very hard on my fast, it didn't happen. I was very honest, and I had worked hard on my feelings. I tried my best to work with the pain of my hunger and thirst. My consolation was that I was making this sacrifice for the Great Spirit and for myself, which was good.

The Fourth Fast

On my fourth fast, I still felt frustrated by my slow progress. I had imagined peace would come to me much more easily. Some very close friends experienced my fourth fast with me. This time I fasted for respect. I fasted to look twice at myself and at all other human beings on this Earth. I lacked the ability to be still because I was eager to experience spiritual insight. We fasted for three days and three nights without food or water. This was a good fast. I felt very intimate with myself. My hunger pains and my thirst for water were not too difficult to deal with and praying came easily. I did my best to show my friends how I was taught to pray in the Native way. After this fast I was much more at peace with myself. I was starting to grow spiritually through the process of fasting.

As I understand it now, I had fasted in the Four Directions. On my first fast I fasted for the North, which is symbolized by movement and caring. On my second fast, I fasted for feelings and vision symbolized in the East. On my third fast, I fasted for relationship and time. It takes time to build relationships with oneself and others, and this is symbolized in the South. On my fourth fast, I fasted for respect and reason. This is symbolized in the West.

As noted above, the Four Directions are symbolized in colour by white for North, red for East, yellow for South, and black for West. These four colours also symbolize the four races of the world. I not only fasted for myself but also for all human beings on this Earth. I still feel good about the sacrifice I made. The Four Directions have a lot of meaning for me today, and my fasting has helped me to grow and to build my inner fire. There is no such thing as a perfect spiritual life. I believe my spiritual progress is slow but it is clean and honest, and that gives me a lot of satisfaction. My struggle for spiritual growth has begun.

The Sweatlodge

The sweatlodge is a divine gift from the Creator. The purpose of the lodge is to purify our mind, body, and spirit through this form of prayer. It is a very sacred place to be because it is the experience that is important rather than the intellectual understanding of the ritual itself. Perhaps that is why little, if anything, has been written about it. However, we are coming of age as a people, so to speak, and the time to integrate our understanding on the intellectual and spiritual levels is at hand, so I offer a brief description here.

I never really experienced a sweatlodge until I arrived at the end of my first fast. I was invited by my Spiritual Elders to my first sweat in the mountains near Calgary. I was in a weakened state of mind as I had not eaten or drunk water for four days. For some inexplicable reason, I felt strong in my heart.

The sweatlodge came to the Anishnabe by way of a little boy. The little boy, in our Creation story, named everything on Earth Mother, including humans. He named all the animals, all the birds, all the fish, all the insects, and all the plants, trees, and lakes. Aside from these naming ceremonies, he also introduced us to the Seven Grandfathers. These Grandfathers reside in our sweatlodges and help us heal our weak minds.

To honour that little boy is to honour the story of our humble beginnings that, in part, answer the mysteries of life. While many First Nations teachings have been eradicated from the face of the Earth, all people at one point in their lives ask the fundamental question, "Why am I here?" The Elders' response is to apply the teachings of the Seven Grandfathers to clarify where you stand. The application of these teachings of the Seven Grandfathers implicitly instructs us to honour all of Creation, and in a very real sense the honouring means to "serve each other."

"That is why we are here." The Elder Eddy Belrose introduced me to the lodge by sharing the purpose of life. He said, "If we recognize each other's spirit and humanity we begin to empower each other."

Since then, my life has been empowered to serve my fellow human beings and for these very reasons it enables me to gather my strength. It prepares me for the day when I will exit the West Door and join Spirit World. Spiritual empowerment is used to strengthen your own fire. We need strength to travel from the West Door to the home of the Creator and the only way home that I know of, is through the Elders' teaching of cedar. Cedar is the medicine that helps our people travel in the Spirit World to the home of the Creator.

We are straying away from the teachings that have been given to us. Many of our young people do not pray and give thanks. Our priorities are confused at best, and our leaders are young in their traditional knowledge. They need to know how to listen to themselves first and hear the voice of the Creator through the voices of the Grandmothers and Grandfathers, as well as their ancestors who are in Spirit World. It is all connected to give us direction and maintain balance, which we access through the sweatlodge. That is the essence of the sweatlodge.

First Nations people say the sweatlodge represents the womb of our birth mother, Mother Earth, and the universe. All human beings come from the womb. We all arrive on a river of water when we descend from the womb. One of our first gifts of life is derived from the West Door, which represents water. You will never be purer than at the moment you are born or humbler than when you are within your last breath of life. We are connected to our Earth Mother through the blood and water of her womb.

Many people on Turtle Island take water for granted. As you know, water sustains all of life, even for the most extreme bigot. By that I mean a person who does not understand the intricate sacredness of life through dependence on all of our life supports: air, food, sun, water, earth, and fire. Several generations ago when my great grandfather washed and drank from the water of White River, near Wawa, Ontario, he left his imprint upon it. We are, essentially, still connected through that water. Water is the First Nations' definition of unconditional love. Water gives without beginning or end. It just is. It is our responsibility to secure the health of the elements that feed us goodness and life for future generations.

In our teachings, women have the primary responsibility to care for water because this life force enables them to give birth. The human race is conceived from the fire of man and woman and delivered from the wombs of our mothers. Within the lodge it is totally dark. The idea is to revisit the place of our humble beginnings and experience a form of spiritual rebirth. The need to control subsides and learning to accept yourself "with all of your baggage," as we say nowadays, begins. Baggage implies the egocentric tendencies that knock us off the good road.

The Elders say that the drum is the voice of our Earth Mother and we need to hear that voice if we are to succeed on our healing journey. That leads me to believe that the sweatlodge embodies the universe and all that it implies. To take care of the Earth and the community of life we need to remember the teachings of the little boy. He handed all the gifts of knowledge that he received from the

Seven Grandfathers to us so that we would know where we stood in the scope of the universe.

These Grandfathers implicitly give us direction to resolve the conflicts of our inner demons. The little boy was anguished. He had witnessed the conflict with his own family and between the clans that warred within each other. He decided that he must do something about all this fighting. His desperation led him to the bush where he fasted and prayed for answers. It was then that the Creator took pity on him and took him into Her home. There the little boy saw a dome-shaped structure whose door faced East toward a sacred fire. The sacred fire represents the Creator who is inside every human being. Our responsibility is to keep that fire alive. The door faced East because he was there to renew himself. Renewal is a primary teaching of the East Door.

This little boy was experiencing a powerful vision when he hesitated to go into the lodge. The first Grandfather to beckon the child forward was the Grandfather of *Wisdom*. Wisdom teaches us to translate the teachings of the lodge into practical daily uses. When we maintain wisdom it guides us naturally towards love. To know the Grandfather of Love is to have inner peace.

Love helps us to understand humility. The Grandfather of *Humility* is the acceptance that we are only a small part of Creation. We in essence resemble a leaf on a tree that dies and is reborn according to the season. The fourth Grandfather the little boy met was *Bravery*. To be brave is to face your enemy without fear. That includes your internal demons. We welcome challenges because theory alone doesn't work on this good Earth. *It is in difficult times that you are called upon to act out of your goodness.* Your benevolence enables you to practise the Grandfather of your *Honesty* without fear. That is why it is important to have the Grandfather of *Respect*, so that you may respect yourself first, and then you can respect others. We hold the Grandfather of *Truth* the virtue by which you become familiar with the six previous Grandfathers. Be true to yourself and to everything you do. This now completes the council of Grandfathers whom you are a part of in the lodge.

If life were a maze, the first phase of your life would be to orient yourself blindly towards the centre of your being. Having reached the centre you would have to take the time to sort out where you stood. Having found your truth you would then have to share it with others. This was the task that faced the little boy. The Grandfathers instructed him to take his vision and recreate the sacred ways on Turtle Island. From time and memory, because this little boy respected his own vision, we now have a way of solving conflicts within and among ourselves.

I was powerless when I was drinking, and my life fell apart. At other times in my life I was reasonable and sane. But when it came to drinking alcohol, I lost control. Once I put the cork back in the bottle, however, I contemplated my powerlessness over the situation. Elders assist us as impartial witnesses to our internal matrixes and know exactly where we have to step if we truly want to liberate ourselves.

They said, "If you want to develop and work from the point of the centre, you must reflect on your past and do a thorough self-examination of all of your weaknesses and strengths." For that revelation I had to ask the Creator and the Grandfathers to help me articulate my inner confusion so that I could change a negative into a positive.

The Grandfathers can be understood in terms of spirit guides who possess all the knowledge of the universe. They are available to everyone. Sometimes they may plant thoughts in our minds to give us direction and guidance. These thoughts always make the utmost sense. Their purpose is to help us in our spiritual evolution. I believe the terms Grandfather and Grandmother were coined eons ago when the traditions were being laid down because they were words that people connected with the wisdom of ages.

To advance in my spiritual quest I offered my tobacco to the Elders. In essence I trusted them with my life. Tobacco is always used as a binding offering. It is the first gift that the Creator gave to implement the teachings. After all I had been through I hesitated at the door of the lodge. I wasn't scared. I was humbled by its sacredness. I was wrapped in a huge comfortable towel and it provided me with security. When the sweatlodge door closed I could feel the breath of the Creator. Her force was emitting heat through the Grandfathers that are represented by the rocks. My heartbeat increased as I anticipated the arrival of the spirits. I felt my entire body being consumed by the heat within the sweatlodge. Although inches from me, I was unaware of the people seated next to me.

The Elder began his prayers and I heard his voice very clearly and distinctly as he proceeded with the teachings. In the darkness the spirit of the Bear gave him a firm hug. I was shocked yet pleased to be singled out. I could hear his breath in my ear and feel his paws on my back. The sensation didn't frighten me. What scared me was when he ripped the towel from my waist and flung it across the lodge. (I had inadvertently removed this towel from a Holiday Inn.) When the people seated beside me felt the impact, everyone screamed, except for the Elder.

In a curt voice he asked, "Where did this towel come from?"

I meekly whispered, "The Holiday Inn."

"Never, never bring anything stolen into the lodge! Spirit seriously frowns upon anything stolen," the Elder scolded.

Needless to say, I never take anything from hotels anymore, except the bar of soap graciously laid out for my use. The Bear in one sweeping motion ripped the dark shadow that had consumed me for twenty-six years. I'm not speaking of the towel now but of the force of my addiction.

After we finished the ceremony the Elder turned towards me and said, "You will never drink again. The Bear has healed you."

Not knowing what else to say or believe I merely gave thanks. Everything had come full circle and my original prayers of cleansing had been answered. For the first time in my life I gave sincere thanks to the Creator. The little boy instructs us to say *Miigwetch* (thank you) each time we leave the lodge. That day I was thanking the Creator for my life and to this day I offer my tobacco in gratitude for every waking moment.

After suffering twenty-six years in a self-imposed prison I realized that fasting and questing were not punishments but a way to liberate myself. When my prison walls broke, I was able to give thanks sincerely from my heart and give freely of my rekindled fire. I served by receiving my spiritual rock and my sacred pipe. When I was given my pipe from the Elder I was told, "Drop everything you're doing and step forward. You will conduct the pipe ceremonies the way the Elders have taught you."

When I perform pipe ceremonies I invite the Creator, the Grandmothers, and the Grandfathers, including the Seven Grandfathers, to heal our shadows. Perhaps that is why I had to suffer so much to understand what liberation meant. I was compelled to walk on the dark side first. I hope to shed light on the darkness of humanity's shortcomings, exemplified so horrendously nowadays in our materialistic greed.

When I was on the streets and had no food or shelter, people looked at me with contempt. If you were on the margins with no home, broken promises, and systematic rejection by government and people who have no understanding except to be critical of your external appearance, you would suffer the pain of my people.

First and foremost I invite all my red brothers and sisters into our home, the sweatlodge, and all the sacred medicines. Our prayers help sustain the Earth Mother and all who live on Her. You belong to Her and no power can take away that which was given to us by the Creator. You are invited into our home to share your spirit with me and to heal by the hands of the Seven Grandfathers.

The heated rock in the sweat is one and the same with the rock of our pipes. The rock is the oldest Grandfather and is very strong. Before the Creator made trees, lakes, ground, and grass, She made the rock. Our connection to the rock represents strength. When we smoke the pipe we offer our good intentions to the Creator. You are either in balance or you are not, and it takes strength to walk the good road every day.

The second teaching of the rock reminds us to make decisions for ourselves. Taking responsibility means making choices that you can live with. The third thing it reminds us of is command. We can command ourselves to be good or fearful people. Finally, the fourth teaching of the rock is to control those very fears that can consume us if we let them.

The Struggle
for Understanding

Self-restraint is closely related to control. There are times when I feel I am right and someone else is wrong. An issue may feel black and white to me, but I can never know what kind of pressure the other person is under. I cannot know what it is like to be that person; therefore I have no right to try to control anyone else's decisions. If the problem is alcohol, I try to explain how drink can destroy, and I describe what happened to me because of my drinking. I offer my knowledge but I leave the decision making to the other person. My hope is to be an example, that is all. I am only responsible for my own sobriety and my own happiness, and I have no right to control other people, or offer solutions to their problems. That is how the rock teaches me faith: faith in my powers, my decisions, my command, and my control over myself.

There are two aspects of ourselves that we must all take care of, or run the risk of living a life of imbalance. These are our external self and our inner self. The external is the image we project to the outside world, sometimes called our "persona." We cultivate our external self in many ways, such as through dress, language, education, our likes and dislikes, the different ways we project ourselves at different times, etc. Cultvating our inner self, however, means cultivating our ability to use common sense to feel our way through life. While "common sense" sounds like a simple thing, something everyone has, it is in fact something we should not take for granted. We build and nurture our common sense with the help of the spirits. Our inner self is more like the impulse to do the right thing, a direction we get from living according to the Grandfathers.

My ability to feel had been suppressed for several decades. My vision was blurred by alcohol. I was engulfed in the negative sound of my inner critic and had forgotten the voice of reason. There was nothing comforting in knowing the smell of my own body rotting under my own nose. The vulgarity and nonsense that spewed from my mouth was tremendous. I was drowning myself in alcohol and I could not feel or touch life from any other position but that of a dead man. Surprisingly, my body was receptive to my attempts at reviving my broken spirit. Awakening from my twenty-year slumber brought the dream of hope back into life.

Out of sight, out of mind.
We take care of our inner life through personal reflection. Personal reflection is obtained by using the Hub, Medicine Wheel, sweetgrass, and the sacred pipe. Through reflection we change and grow spiritually. It has been said that many Native people avoid looking you in the eye, and that this

is an indication of their feelings of inferiority. This is not so. It is simply a cultural trait based on respect. The only time you can know whether people feel inferior is by their self-disclosure. There were many times when I felt inferior in front of great men like the Elders. The Elders from the "Four Skies" taught me the value of seeing goodness in other people. So when I meet other human beings, I always use my eyes to look for goodness in them. Whether I am meeting them for the first time or the tenth time, it doesn't matter. I use my vision to observe goodness through their behaviour.

Listen if you will.

The next thing I tried to develop were my caring ears. I work really hard at trying to hear when someone talks to me. I find you have to really concentrate to listen well. Using my ears to listen helps me to establish a relationship with the people I talk with. I not only listen to the words they use to convey a message to me but I listen to the feelings behind the words so I am able to understand them better. Sometimes when I meet and listen to someone, envy gets in the way. When I envy another person I'm not using my ears. When I give envy power I am not trying to balance myself by using my ears and my eyes in a caring way. If I look hard enough and long enough, I will see some good in that person. Then my feelings of inferiority will slowly diminish or fade away and my envy will be reduced. If I use my eyes and ears in my encounters with others I will be able to establish more satisfying relationships with people.

Honesty, the "best medicine."

When I was drinking I always tried to con people for money so I could buy a drink. It was hard to tell the truth because I wanted a drink so badly. Even after I sobered up it was very hard to tell the truth about myself and what I was doing. I had conned and manipulated people for so many years that it became my way of life. So it took a lot of extra effort to be honest with myself and with others. For example, after I sobered up, sometimes people asked me what I did for a living. I felt ashamed to tell them that I worked for the government, although I had absolutely nothing to be ashamed of. I put in an honest day's work for an honest day's pay, so why should I feel ashamed? This shame was a symptom of a much deeper problem. I had problems with dignity. I could find no satisfaction within myself. It takes time to build honesty from within. I had to come to terms with my profession, my skills, and my being and accept them. I was not comfortable with who I was. I started to change my attitude about where I worked; to take pride in my work, and to care about the work I was doing. Once I started to take pride in who I was and what I was doing, my honesty became stronger. As a matter of fact, I felt good about where I worked because I knew I was doing the right thing. I did not compromise my honesty while at work.

The taste of enlightened speech.

Once I have identified issues, I develop a caring plan. I try to live my talk. As the saying goes, "I walk the talk." But sometimes, even if I have a plan, if I do not trust the other person, I become jealous. To become jealous is to become possessive and unwilling to share. Then I have to ask the Creator and the Grandfathers to help me with my jealousy, to take away the jealousy within me. The spiritual Grandfathers have taught me a lot. As my relationship with the Spirit World gets stronger, I become less jealous and possessive because I am humbled by their presence, which helps me accept myself as I am. I am beginning to understand what the Elder told me when he said that I had to learn about how to live with the spirits. I need to use my eyes, my ears, my mind, and my behaviour – that is, my external self, in a caring way. I find it is working for me and I feel good about myself.

Today, I have the power of choice to speak good words or harmful words. Today, I have the power to listen; the power to listen to feelings. Today, I have the power to use my eyes and see good things in myself and others. I never had this power when I was drinking. It is only by the grace of the Great Spirit that the Elders, who taught me this wisdom, came into my life. Today, I have the power to use my mind to make honest and kind decisions for myself and others.

Today I remember my daughter's poem of fifteen years ago. She called it "The Destroyer" because she knew the power of alcohol to destroy.

You think I am harmless

I have the power

I have the power to destroy ...

It took me some years to catch up to my young daughter's wisdom.

The touchstone of healing.

There are times when we use our minds to identify concerns or issues that another person has to deal with. If I have a clear mind, I am able to identify these issues and to deal with them. But sometimes resentment gets in the way. I may give power to resentment even if it is not directed at the person I am talking with. It could be an old resentment I have not dealt with that wells up inside me, triggered by something the person says or does. I try to balance myself by asking the Creator and the Grandfathers to take away my resentment.

We call good spirits "Grandfathers" because they are very kind, like my grandfather. I never heard him mention or say anything bad about another person. I cannot remember him ever expressing resentment. The spirit Grandfathers always give, and they ask for nothing in return. This is what some people call unconditional love. My grandfather in Mobert was always giving and never asked for anything in return. Grandmother was the same. They were both very good people. They had done many good things around Mobert and they provided good examples for me and the rest of my family. They were also very spiritual people in the Catholic church. I try to follow their example. In this way they helped me to clear my mind and I am able to deal with issues a lot better. My resentments are getting smaller and less frequent. No longer do I resent, or re-feel, the past as much as I used to. My mind is much healthier these days. It is not clogged up with a lot of negative attitudes.

The first honest and kind decision that I made for myself was to admit that I was powerless over alcohol and that I had become insane because of my drinking. My behaviour was completely out of control. When I admitted my weakness, I started to grow in strength. Self-control began to develop within me. I now choose to direct myself and to relate positively to others. But the hardest thing for me is to control myself when I am under pressure. I have many pressures today. I have pressures at work, pressures to do the right thing, pressures to be honest when I would prefer not to be ... I am satisfied with the degree of self-control I have today, but there is plenty of room for improvement, especially when I lose my temper and things get out of hand. Generally, my biggest problem with control is that I tend to want to control other people's decisions. I need to learn to hold back my power of persuasion and my opinions when they are inappropriate. My strength has improved because I can restrain myself better than I used to. I have better control over my five little rascals – not caring, feelings of inferiority, envy, resentment, and jealousy.

I also had to work on honesty within my relationships, especially with Laura. I had to tell her how I felt about things, my fears and hopes. It is not always pleasant to tell your partner about your fears. My relationship with Laura helped me grow because I learned about myself through her. Through her kindness, I learned how to appreciate myself. I was also determined to be honest with my good friend Sheila, the mother of our children, and with our two children. I explained to them that, even though I sobered up, I was still immature in many ways, and that I was not as strong as I wanted to be. It was difficult to admit my immaturity.

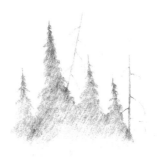

The Spiritual Path

The tree is the symbol of honesty in our tradition. If you take a walk in the forest you will notice there are many kinds of trees. There are white trees, yellow trees, black trees, and red trees. There are trees of many shades of colour. Trees symbolize the four races of the world. Within these four races there is intermarriage and people born from these marriages have different shades of colour. They are not pure white, or pure red. Also, if you walk in the bush, you will see trees of different shapes and sizes. Some are tall, some are crooked, some are twisted. They represent all the people of the world. Walking the "Sweetgrass Road" helps me to be tall and straight like a tall straight tree. When I go into the bush, I can read my behaviour. My behaviour will be reflected back to me by what I see. If I am living dishonestly I will notice a tree that is crooked, and that tree will represent me. But if I strive for an honest life, and progress with honesty, I will find a straight tree and that tree will be me. I find a lot of meaning in trees.

When I first met my teacher, Eddy, I was very abrupt with him and cynical about his teachings. I mocked him,

"If you believe you can talk to trees, that's your prerogative. I'm going out for a drink," I said to him. I could not care less about the pipe, sweetgrass, or other Native ceremonies. My impression of the Native culture and its special relationship to Nature was extremely negative. I was openly hostile towards the traditional concepts and beliefs. My mind and heart were cold. I did not know how to receive the Elders, or how to listen. Nor did I have the slightest idea of how to use the information that they were willingly sharing with me.

I left Mobert in a hopeless condition some twenty-seven years ago. I returned to Mobert sober and have thankfully remained so since August 1983. My main purpose in going back was to bring the sweetgrass to the reserve and to reintroduce traditional Native concepts to those who were interested in re-examining Native values. More importantly, I wanted to see how these traditional values could be applied to today's problems. My culture embraces universal values that are treasured by all peoples of the world. Honesty and kindness are central to all major cultures and religions. However, the traditional Native culture expresses these values in a unique way. All of our values are expressed through Nature, and then Nature teaches us how to behave and how to conduct our lives. The trick is to learn how to read and understand Nature. I found that it takes a long time to get close to Nature. I feel that I am not yet as close as I would like to be. Although I have gone through various ceremonies and many discussions with our Elders I still feel I am only seeing the tip of the iceberg. The most valuable thing that I received from understanding our culture is a perspective on my life that is more comprehensive and mature than it was during those years when I was drinking.

Spiritual growth is an intense process and it is not always comfortable. I had to admit deep down inside my heart that I was very weak. I had to admit it not only to myself but to another human being and to the Creator. The process of admitting my weaknesses and character flaws helped me to rediscover my spiritual strength. I do not believe there is any mystery to allowing the spirits near. Love and hate cannot live comfortably in the same house. What I have been doing over the years was to admit my hate and ask the Great Spirit to remove hatred from me. Once I had removed these feelings of hate my stress and anxiety levels began to reduce considerably. Besides working on my spiritual strength, I have tried to improve my physical condition. In order to have a sound, healthy mind, you need a healthy body. If your body is sick, your mind will eventually become sick. So I do my best to exercise and to eat nutritious meals. I have had to learn a whole new pattern of living. When I was drinking, I had little or no discipline. Changing the pattern has not been easy because I had lived a very undisciplined lifestyle for so long. Now I try to live on a more scheduled routine and this takes time.

I am grateful today. I'm thankful to have spent quality time with the Elders whose Spirit World was gracious enough to guide me. It was through their example and care that I was able to receive the traditional teachings and learn how to use them for my own benefit. It has been a good journey for me. My struggle for the relighting of my personal power has been a tough road, but I would not have had it any other way. My new-found power has helped me to open up my mind and to understand my feelings. It has certainly helped me with my spiritual development and it is all because of the Elders' patience and belief in me. Their perseverance and strength to preserve our spiritual beliefs and fight for me is moving. I am forever grateful for the Elders. The struggle for spiritual power to control myself and the struggle for the power to make sacrifices is never ending. Realistically, I will always be learning from my weaknesses so I can make better decisions for myself.

It is hard to see the world correctly through the curve of your arm as you chug yet another bottle of booze or a glass of poison that you wouldn't have your dog drink. I am learning how to be grateful. That was one feeling I never had when I was drinking.

Miigwech to my father.
My father was a past chief of Pic Mobert First Nation and his teachings were of purity. "Whatever you do in life, my son, do not compromise your honesty. It is always good to be honest." This was his legacy to me. I disregarded his gift for many, many years, but eventually I recaptured his teaching on the importance of honesty. Dad taught that kindness could also work against you. Your kindness has to be balanced. "If you are too kind and generous, people may take advantage of you."

I found this to be a very useful lesson. People can become too dependent on your kindness. As the ancient parable has it, if I went fishing everyday and I gave my neighbour a fish as an expression of my kindness, after a time, he would come to expect the fish and he would not go out and hunt for fish himself. Soon he would become dependent upon my fish for food; he would not have gained the dignity or work habits to go out and fish for himself. However, if I took him to the lake and I taught him how to fish and harvest food, it would be more productive and I would have showed my kindness. My father passed away on 1 July 1982. Throughout my childhood, I remember that my Dad was always honest with us, with his wife and all his friends.

When I was drinking I became totally dependent upon alcohol. For many years alcohol helped me to cope with my problems and my life in general. I believe people who gave me drinks were not helping my situation. Without knowing it they were contributing to my problem. I was dependent upon alcohol and I had a sick mind. My father showed me tough kindness when he asked me to leave shortly after I lost my arm. He did not want me to become too dependent on his kindness. He taught me independence the hard way.

Miigwech to my birth mother Mabel.
As a child living in a remote community, we had no electricity in our home. My mother spent most of her life cooking meals, cleaning our clothes, washing the floors,

and helping us to take baths. She worked very hard to make sure we always had enough food and clean clothes, and a warm place to live. When I reflect on her caring I see it as an expression of her kindness towards her children, and her kindness towards herself. She used to sing songs to us. She had a great sense of humour and she was always teasing my dad. My mother lived her kindness. I wish I had had more time with her. The memory of her spiritual life has a great influence on me today.

Miigwech to my grandparents and ancestors.
My grandparents on my dad's side of the family were thoughtful people. Granddad always made sure Grandma had enough supplies, and they both provided us with love and affection. He was very kind towards the children. My grandfather passed away when he was in his fifties. My grandmother was a very gracious lady. She had a sense of humour right until her death. She died at the age of seventy-nine. I never heard her complain about my grandfather's passing away but she did mention she was lonely several times. She was not afraid to show her feelings. Grandmother had dignity and accepted her needs and her right to express her feelings. She lived by her principles of honesty and kindness and taught from her heart. I feel honoured and humbled to have known people who have walked the good road. Every time an Elder passes so does a large portion of our history.

Miigwech to the animals.
The animals have given me many of the teachings. They

know how to share and be responsible for their young ones. They never abuse their young. I am grateful for the way they use creation. They never mistreat creation like I did when I was drinking. I am grateful for the way animals teach me how to be a companion. They know how to be affectionate towards each other. Today, I try to be affectionate.

Finally, animals can teach me about sacrifice. They give up their lives so we can use them for food. They teach me that I should make sacrifices in my own life. At one time I would not have made a sacrifice for anyone. I was too greedy and jealous to think about making sacrifices. I did not even know what the word meant. Since I have sobered up I have made some sacrifices. A good sacrifice is quick, pure, and simple. It is better not to tell anyone about it, but just keep it to yourself. The purer the sacrifice, the closer you get to the Creator. Before I knew what sacrifice meant, I would make sure that the person I was helping knew that I was the one helping them. I told everyone else that I was helping as well. Of course, this was not really a sacrifice. It was only a way of showing off. I was a great one for showing off when I was drinking and before I sobered up, I never made any honest sacrifices. I am grateful to the animals and their teaching of sacrifice.

Animals teach me affection. Your little house-dog is a very affectionate animal. If you call him, he will always come to you wagging his tail. He will rub his body against your legs. If you get angry with him, a few seconds later he will forgive you. I have learned from the house-dog. I try to practise his way of showing affection.

Animals also teach me not to abuse sex. For instance, loons mate for life. They are loyal to each other. There are many other animals who do not abuse sex. The Elders refer to sex as creation and it is because of my parents' expression of kindness that I was created. From what I remember, my parents never abused sex. They lived according to the principles of loyalty and fidelity because of their honesty. But that is not my point. Animals can teach us many things if we have the courage to admit our weaknesses.

When I was a child I was taught by the school system to feel superior to the animals. Today, I do not look at it that way. I see goodness in animals and I can learn from them. The Elders taught me that animals can teach us if we know how to observe and understand their behaviour.

Animals can also teach us companionship. If you ever drive by a farm you will notice how horses stand beside each other. They seem to cuddle up and they rub their necks against each other. You can tell they are very close and enjoy each other's company. Their companionship is a model of how I could relate to my companions and friends.

Miigwetch for the ability to receive goodness.
When I was drinking I could never receive. I did not know how to receive a gift. Today, that has all changed. I now understand that receiving helps to enhance self-love because I am able to get close to Nature and to the Creator and to other people.

Miigwetch for sobriety.
Today, I belong to the fellowship of men and women who

try to live a spiritual life. Their main aim is to stay sober. They embrace the universal values of honesty and kindness towards themselves and others. I identify with these men and women, and they are a big source of help to me. I use this fellowship and the Elders' teachings to stay on the right path. They are my anchor. They keep me from going to extremes in any direction so that I can maintain my balance. Once, I met a man who talked of honesty as if it were an absolute. Honesty itself must be balanced. You should never interfere with other people's boundaries and safety.

Miigwetch for tolerance and perseverance.

As I learned to grow and to like myself, I became more tolerant of others. This is a wonderful feeling. A human being is too complex to be assessed as a constant because our moods change very quickly. We may remember a particular act of kindness or humiliation, but that does not mean that that person is constantly kind or abusive. I find that in my sober life my moods change quickly and they are too complex to analyze or understand. Over time I have become more stable. I am able to accept my mood changes with the help of the fellowship and my dependency upon the Great Spirit.

Miigwetch for my life today.

I am grateful for my life today, and I feel that I have been reborn with the help of the Elders and the traditional Native culture. Being reborn is a painful process. It is no different than the pain little babies feel when coming out of their mother's womb. It is painful, but it has also been incredibly satisfying. I am able to live my life now in a decent manner.

The four virtues of sharing, honesty, kindness, and building spiritual strength are part of my basic values today. While I was drinking I valued greed, hate, revenge, and personal ambition. I accomplished these values at the expense of others. I continue working on changing that to a healthy way of living. This is part of balance – learning to change my basic values.

Miigwetch for the awareness of boundaries.
I try not to judge other people, although I catch myself doing it at times. I try to accept people because within the circle of life we are all equal.

Miigwetch to all nations.
The sun shines equally for all families of people. It shines for the black people, the yellow people, the white people, and the red people. It shines for all the animals, all plants, and all living things and creation.

Miigwetch for the sacrifices.
The sun gives light and heat unconditionally and I try to follow that example; I try to give unconditionally. It is really hard sometimes, but it works. Unconditional caring is beautiful. The moment I attach conditions to my caring and giving, it is no longer giving and sharing from my heart. When there is a price attached it does not work. The best sacrifices are the small ones. Once you start to brag

about all your sacrifices it no longer means anything because you just want to look good and puff up your ego.

Miigwetch for the sacred teachings.
I am grateful for the Hub, the Four Sacred Directions, the sweatlodge, and my pipe.

Miigwetch to the forest and to the grass.
Whenever you walk through rough bush, where there are a lot of steep little hills and underbrush, similar to the bush that you find around the north shore of Lake Superior, all of a sudden you may come across a delightful little meadow and when your feet touch the grass it feels very soft. It feels good to walk without tripping over the heavy underbrush. The grass teaches me kindness like my grandmother taught me kindness. She lived the word. I have never heard her say unkind things about anyone. I use sweetgrass to pray. The grass reminds me of my own kindness.

Miigwetch to all plants.
I am grateful for all the plants. If I have good food, I have good feelings. If I eat a lot of junk food I do not feel good. Today, I realize that good food helps me to have good feelings.

Miigwetch to the standing people.
I am grateful for the Tree Nation. Some trees are crooked, some trees are tall and straight. I am tall and straight because inside I feel I am living an honest life.

Miigwetch to the stone nation.
I am grateful for the rock. The rock symbolizes my powers
– the power to think, to make decisions, to command, and
to control myself. I am grateful today that I can learn from
the rock.

Miigwetch to the winds of change.
I am grateful for the air I breathe. It never occurred to me
to think about the power of air before. Air helps me to
move and if I care, my movement will be done in a caring
way. I will know how to move in a good way.

Miigwetch to sister water.
I am also grateful for water today. When I was drinking I
drank firewater that ate up my insides to a point where my
liver would stop functioning if I continued to drink. Today I
drink clean water. Water helps me to see; water is in my eyes.
Three-quarters of my body is water. I have learned to look
twice at the things around me and to reason in a good way.

Miigwetch to Grandfather Sun.
I am grateful for the sun. The sun helps me to see and it
doctors my mind through the optic nerves. When I was
drinking I did not like to be in the sun because it bothered
my eyes. I wanted to be in dark dingy barrooms. Today, I
like the sun.

Miigwetch to Grandmother Moon.
The sister of the sun, our sister the moon, takes care of
all the females on the Earth Mother. Without her there

would be serious imbalances and for their selfless work I am grateful.

Miigwetch to Mother Earth.
She nourishes all of life including our lodges where she provides "Earth" strength and "female" strength. For that I love you.

Miigwetch to the Creator.
These are all gifts from the Creator. The Creator gave me a mind to use, to think and make decisions, and the ability to keep an open mind. I think of my body as a temple, as a gift from the Creator, and it is up to me to look after my body, not to destroy it with alcohol. It is a very precious and valuable gift.

Miigwetch to all my relations.
In this book I have merely touched on the basics of the Teachings. There are some things that must be kept secret to maintain their sacredness. Only when you decide to embark upon your own spiritual journey will you understand the full meaning of the Teachings. The Lone Ranger signed off with his signature, "High, ho, Silver, away!" I will make do with what I have and share with all of you the call to Nature that I now practise on a daily basis. I have no claim to it so please feel free to use it as your own.

*Miigwetch gzhemnidoo./*Thank-you Great Spirit.
From your humbled child, Herb.

Glossary

Cedar: Cedar is called Tree of Light by the Ojibway people. This tree has the capacity to shine a light for the spirits in the Spirit World when they are travelling from the west door of the lodge to the home of the Creator. It is considered a very sacred tree by Aboriginal people who follow the traditional way.

Eagle Feather: The eagle feather represents balance.

Elder: An Elder is an Aboriginal person who is close to the Creator and the Spirit World. Elders conduct healing ceremonies, such as sweatlodge and pipe ceremonies, fasts, and other healing ceremonies from other Aboriginal nations. An Elder is also an individual who has good balance and is not affected by the five rascals – inferiority, envy, resentment, not caring, and jealousy. An Elder is a complete, kind, and gentle person who has the capacity to fix and heal illnesses.

Fire: The fire is seen as a spark that lives in all human beings.

Hub: The Hub is a Cree understanding of the human personality. It can be explained according to the good and dark sides of life. The good side is represented by the good spirits such as Naniboozoo, characterized by good feelings, good relationships, respect, caring, and listening to oneself. The Windigo represents the dark side of life – inferiority, envy, resentment, not caring, and jealousy. The Windigo controls all spiritual, physical, and mental diseases in the world.

Medicine Wheel: The Medicine Wheel is an ancient tool used by our ancestors to explain our world view. It also helped them organize their medicines, animals, birds, and plants in a systematic fashion. It helped them to understand life in accordance with nature as we understand it today.

Red: If you look towards the east in the morning the sky is red; for the Crees, red represents renewal, where life begins. The Turtle Spirit in the East represents the healing of the hearts and feelings of the red people. When we are in our sweatlodges we ask the Turtle Spirit to mend our broken hearts and broken feelings.

Yellow: As the sun travels from east to west, at midday it faces south. The sun has always been a timepiece; time is measured through the four seasons of the Medicine Wheel and the hunt was organized around the seasons. The yellow represents Giinu, the Golden Eagle. The

Golden Eagle delivers all our thoughts and prayers in the sweatlodge to the Creator. The Creator then responds to our requests for guidance and protection.

Black: If you look at the dark clouds in the spring, you know from experience that they will more than likely bring rain. Water is represented in the West, where the Thunderbird sits. We ask the Thunderbird to heal the dark side of our inner lives, represented by the five rascals.

White: White represents the North. The North wind can move anything on the planet. The Bear, which sits in the North, is the ultimate healer, able to heal any physical, spiritual, or mental illnesses.

Green: Green represents Mother Earth. The Earth nutures all of life and at the centre of the Earth is a huge fire. The fire is getting weaker and earth is very sick. According to our Elders it is five minutes to midnight.

Pipe: The pipe represents the heart of the people. We use our pipes to communicate with the Creator. It is my understanding that all nations on Turtle Island use the pipe. The pipe is explained in many ways by different nations.

Sage: Sage is a plant that is used around healing circles and sweatlodges and is considered by many to be a female medicine. It cleans the mind, body, and spirit of those involved in the ceremonies.

Sweetgrass: Sweetgrass is used in ceremonies and represents the hair of Mother Earth. It is a very sacred plant that weaves the mind, body, and spirit into one. It has a strong healing capacity and it cannot be broken once an individual uses the plant with sincerity and honesty.

Tobacco: Tobacco represents kindness. The smoke that emanates from our pipes represents the kind thoughts that we send to our Creator.

Water: Water is introduced to the fetus in our mother's womb and life begins with water. When we are born we come out of the womb on a river of water. That is why babies have no fear of water. Water is also the blood of Mother Earth.

McGill-Queen's Indigenous and Northern Studies
(In memory of Bruce G. Trigger)
Sarah Carter and Arthur J. Ray, Editors

McGill-Queen's Indigenous and Northern Studies
(In memory of Bruce G. Trigger)
Sarah Carter and Arthur J. Ray, Editors